Teaching Math, Science, and Technology in Schools Today

Guidelines for Engaging Both Eager and Reluctant Learners

Second Edition

Dennis Adams and Mary Hamm

ROWMAN & LITTLEFIELD EDUCATION
A division of
ROWMAN & LITTLEFIELD
Lanham • Boulder • New York • Toronto • Plymouth, UK

Published by Rowman & Littlefield Education
A division of Rowman & Littlefield
4501 Forbes Boulevard, Suite 200, Lanham, Maryland 20706
www.rowman.com

10 Thornbury Road, Plymouth PL6 7PP, United Kingdom

British Library Cataloguing in Publication Information Available

Library of Congress Cataloging-in-Publication Data

Adams, Dennis, 1947– author.
[Helping students who struggle with math and science]
Teaching math, science, and technology in schools today : guidelines for engaging both eager and reluctant learners / Dennis Adams and Mary Hamm. — Second edition.
pages cm
Revision of: Helping students who struggle with math and science. ?2008.
ISBN 978-1-4758-0903-9 (cloth : alk. paper) — ISBN 978-1-4758-0904-6 (pbk. : alk. paper) — ISBN 978-1-4758-0905-3 (electronic)
1. Mathematics—Study and teaching (Elementary)—United States. 2. Mathematics—Study and teaching (Middle school)—United States. 3. Science—Study and teaching (Elementary)—United States. 4. Science—Study and teaching (Middle school)—United States. 5. Individualized instruction—United States. 6. Mixed ability grouping in education—United States. 7. Group work in education—United States. 8. Cognitive styles in children—United States. I. Hamm, Mary, author. II. Title.
QA135.6.A33 2014
372.7–dc23
2013042445

∞™ The paper used in this publication meets the minimum requirements of American National Standard for Information Sciences Permanence of Paper for Printed Library Materials, ANSI/NISO Z39.48-1992.

Printed in the United States of America

Contents

Preface

Me teach math and science? Those were my worst subjects. I am definitely not a math or science person. As far as technology is concerned, I don't have a clue when somebody mentions Google glasses, algorithms, or big data.
—Anonymous student teacher

When we asked new K–8 teachers about teaching mathematics, science, and technology, many admitted their knowledge of these subjects was limited. Some also said that they only took the minimum number of courses in these subjects required for graduation. Others reported that they had never really understood one or more of these subjects.

It may be asking too much to expect elementary school teachers to deeply know and appreciate the dozens of subjects they have to teach. Still, having a negative attitude toward certain content is bound to have a similar negative impact on students.

You don't have to love math or science to learn or teach it. And you certainly don't have to accept the notion that technology is the key to thinking and knowing about the world. But having a positive attitude sure helps when it comes to generating intellectual curiosity and creative energy.

Learning math, science, and technology is compared by Montreal teacher Eugen Pascu to learning how to drive a car: "First you've got to memorize the rules of the road. Then you've got to apply them to get behind the wheel and actually move the car. . . . You need to learn formulas but you also have to understand how they work. Learn the rules, then see how the rules work" (Peritz, 2013). These ideas apply seamlessly to inquiry and problem solving as well.

Fortunately, there are many experienced teachers who have a fairly positive view of math, science, and technology. In fact, the majority of practicing teachers in our professional development workshops reported that they were reasonably comfortable teaching these subjects. But saying that all experienced teachers are enthusiastic is a stretch.

Educators know that active, participatory, and connected learning is a proven way to help all students experience subjects of which they may not have been fond. Most teachers are familiar with collaborative group work, so there's a relatively easy way for them to approach subjects that students may view as difficult.

Both new and experienced teachers we surveyed show a heightened sense of concern when a discussion turns to engaging students who have trouble with math, science, or technology. Most recognize the fact that reluctant learners may not have been identified as having learning problems. They also know one size doesn't fit all and that there is a need to approach learning in different ways.

There is more and more evidence that having a negative home environment at an early age affects what happens later in school. In fact, adversity can even alter the physical development of a child's brain. So it is little wonder that many are considering implementing preschool programs and reaching out to parents with suggestions.

There is general agreement among educators that work with at-risk children should begin as early as possible. It also makes sense to help all students develop character skills like tenacity, curiosity, and self-control. These skills are central to achieving academic competency.

Unfortunately, all too often, reluctant learners simply don't like math and science—and others think they couldn't be successful in these subjects. Technology is often viewed more positively. But whatever the subject, it seems that poor attitude and poor achievement amplify each other. Clearly, having a positive attitude can help students out of dead-end academic traps.

Equity at the lowest common denominator does more harm than good. Genuine equity must be combined with high academic standards (i.e., excellence) to be successful. Basic skills matter, but teachers must also attend to the students' imagination and ability to ask good questions, solve problems, and generate imaginative ideas.

Questions, engagement, and curiosity are viewed as natural partners for mathematical problem solving, scientific inquiry, and technology-rich learning. With teacher assistance, even students who are having learning problems can move from believing they "can't do" or "don't like" these subjects to having a sense of genuine achievement and confidence.

Teaching Math, Science, and Technology in Schools Today builds on the social nature of learning to provide suggestions for reaching both eager and reluctant learners. The assumption is that instruction that focuses on students' interests and builds on active participatory learning can help generate more interest in any subject.

Clearly, it helps to make math, science, and technology more meaningful to students by connecting them to the questions they ask about their world: Why is the sky blue? How far is my house from school? Is there life on other planets? How do I find the information I need to answer my questions? What problems and solutions do various technologies bring us?

We hope this book opens some imaginative doors to learning so that teachers can provide opportunities for all learners to construct their own knowledge. Ideas and activities for standards-based learning, collaborative inquiry, and active problem solving are part of the package. It is our belief that no one should be sidelined with memorizing basic skills.

In the world outside of school, creative and collaborative engagement is central to mathematical problem solving, scientific inquiry, and technological innovation. So why not use a similar approach for all students in K–8 classrooms?

This book is written in a teacher-friendly style. Special attention is given to the personal and social implications of math, science, and technology. The text is organized in a way that is convenient for school districts that are doing in-service work with elementary and middle school teachers. The book might also serve as a supplementary text for methods classes in mathematics and science education.

Because the technological products of math and science are so important, we pay close attention to the instructional possibilities. It is hoped that the teaching ideas presented will assist teachers as they invite reluctant learners to use technological tools to inquire, discover concepts, and collaboratively explore the interlinking concepts of mathematics, science, and technology.

Technology is a close associate of math and science and an increasingly powerful force both in and out of school. Mathematicians and scientists understand and use a wide range of technological tools. So it makes sense for students to use some of the same tools and methods at an age-appropriate level.

Developing positive attitudes toward math and science goes hand in hand with developing competency. Therefore, this book provides examples of interesting methods and connects them to appropriate technologies and pedagogical approaches that reach across the curriculum. The new Common Core State Standards have influenced this approach.

The overall goal of *Teaching Math, Science, and Technology in Schools Today* is to deepen the collective conversation, challenge thinking, and provide some up-to-date tools for teachers so that they can help reverse the steady erosion of math, science, and technological skills in the general population.

REFERENCE

Peritz, I. "Add Good Teachers, Fractions, Creativity—and Shake." *The Globe and Mail*, December 7, 2013, p. A10.

Chapter One

Helping All Students Learn About Math and Science

In wealthy schools and poor ones, I encountered the same recurring patterns: considerable variation among classrooms in the degree to which students were challenged; an emphasis on procedural knowledge at the expense of analysis, reflection, and understanding; a tendency to focus more on students who were "easy to teach" rather than those who were struggling.

—Richard Elmore

Achieving an adequate national level of numeracy and scientific literacy requires educating all students up to a level of reasonable competency.

It would be wise for every citizen in a democracy to have some idea of where math, science, and their technological offspring are taking us. Take the example of algorithms. They may be thought of as a set of math-related rules for solving a problem in a certain number of steps. They can also be used to tell a computer what to do and *how* to do it.

In the future, any job or activity that can be reduced to an algorithm probably will be. Still, when asked about understanding even one of the many implications of math and science, a surprising number of people in every generation say that their comprehension and appreciation are limited.

The Common Core State Standards recognize the need for changing societal attitudes toward numeracy and literacy. They also suggest that in a wired world, students of all ages need to learn about previously understated dimensions of math and science (Common Core State Standards, 2013).

In spite of their obvious importance, math and science are just about the only topics for which more than a few well-educated adults will freely admit ignorance. Teachers reflect the general population. So it is little wonder that when it comes to teaching these subjects, many of the characteristics of effective instruction fall by the wayside.

Lack of mathematical and scientific interest in the broader society has a corrosive effect on the young. Some simply do not like math and science; others do not think they can be successful. We identify such students as struggling or reluctant learners. Only a few will become mathematicians or scientists, but all need some understanding of math and science to succeed in school, in the workplace, and in life.

Some struggling students may have special needs, but all students in the typical classroom are capable of responding to well-designed active learning approaches (Sherman et al., 2009). The principles of play, purpose, and teamwork can help make good things happen. Clearly, *how* we teach is as important as *what* we teach.

When teaching math and science, asking disaffected learners to reason, solve problems, and maintain a positive disposition may be a tall order. So we should not be surprised when teachers sometimes pay more attention to procedural knowledge than they do to reflection and understanding.

In spite of the difficulties, the primary goal of instruction should be getting every student in the classroom to develop and use the higher-level thinking skills associated with problem solving and inquiry.

Online learning opportunities are developing in ways that offer some intriguing possibilities. But the current crop of online lessons and courses has not helped as much as some had hoped (Dudley-Marling, 2012). The use of shared blogs, for example, may help students get better at working together but seems to have little effect on content mastery.

Active offline collaboration between students at different skill levels can help generate imaginative problem-solving and inquiry experiences for everybody. Like adult experts, all children can profit from the intellectual ferment that happens when they have to collaborate in person and bounce ideas off each other.

No one approach or method of teaching math and science has been found to meet the needs of all students all of the time. But various kinds of active and collaborative learning experiences certainly increase the odds of success.

Although we think of learning as something that happens in school, what happens in the home and social environment is critical. In the final analysis, connecting all students to productive math and science experiences has a lot we developed to help improve student achievement. It builds on students' strengths and can serve as an assessment tool.

EVERYONE NEEDS TO UNDERSTAND MATH AND SCIENCE

The public's failure to understand chance phenomena, statistics, probability, and the nature of numerical assertions opens the way for all manner of belief in nonsense. Perhaps more important, it leads to distortions in the making of public policy.

—John Poulos

The need to understand and use math and science in everyday life has never been greater. Personal satisfaction and confidence come with making wise quantitative decisions, whether it is buying a house, solving problems on the job, choosing health insurance, or voting intelligently. In many ways, mathematics and science are part of our cultural heritage.

Our careers, our workplace, and our community all require a foundation of sound mathematical and scientific knowledge. Although it may not be readily apparent, proficiency in these subjects can open doors to future achievements and sound citizenship. More important than a classroom being online or full of digital devices is having a teacher who appreciates what the new forms of math and science instruction are about.

A quick high-tech fix cannot solve many of the most important human challenges. In fact, thinking that all problems have clean and clear solutions just because we have the technological tools to get rid of them is an illusion. The most genuine problems we face may require drawn-out personal, institutional, and social responses.

Data-enhanced decisions are more than ever part of human decision making. Statisticians and data analysts pay more attention to correlations than human predispositions (Mayer-Schonberger and Cukier, 2013).

Everyone needs to understand mathematics, science, and technology to make decisions about important societal issues in our democracy. Even mass media are not that reliable. Take the example of global warming. For a long time, the story was reported in a way that suggested some scientists took it seriously and some did not. And this was after a large number of the scientists had recognized the reality of the problem.

Advances in medicine have sometimes been reported in another problematic way. Exciting breakthroughs are sometimes reported when only small advancing steps have been taken. Whatever the scientific issue, a better understanding of the mathematical significance of statistical results would help everyone (from the media to the typical student) understand the situation, whatever their age.

When we asked several struggling learners in a sixth-grade class why they were not interested in math and science, many replied that it was "not interesting" or "too difficult," or that it "never made much sense." These explanations and other reasons might be classified as students' personal or environmental situations.

No matter what gets in the way of learning, teachers have to know what to teach and how to teach it. Four or five years of college and continuous professional development help. So do the suggestions and recommendations that can be found in the math and science standards and state and school district guidelines. Even many textbooks are helpful.

Wherever you get instructional ideas, activities often have to be adapted for different students. Everyone in the classroom has to be involved in building knowledge by asking relevant questions, reasoning, making connections, and solving problems.

The Characteristics of Struggling Students

All students of math and science have individual strengths and weaknesses. However, struggling students often have similar learning problems (Armstrong, 2012). Being able to identify individual problems and knowing some helpful teaching strategies certainly helps.

Struggling students may be *passive learners*, who have little motivation or interest in becoming active participants in math and science learning. Some students who struggle may think that math and science achievement is a matter of luck. They may think it is too easy, too difficult, or too boring. They may also believe that achievement in these subjects is beyond their control: "I'm just not good at math" or "Science is boring."

Students with negative feelings about math, science, or technology may prefer not to acknowledge that their lack of success might have something to do with personal discipline, hard work, and persistence. They may mistakenly believe that you succeed in math and science through some combination of luck and level of intelligence.

The home and school environments matter a great deal; if poor achievement is expected, then that is the most likely result. Whatever the reason, when students are discouraged or disinterested, their ability to move forward is limited.

Teachers can learn to do a good job with struggling students without simplifying problems or always telling them exactly what to do. It is important to get learners actively involved in interesting and relevant situations. So the teacher has to encourage reluctant learners to construct ideas and communicate their thoughts.

Graphic wall charts can help individual students see how they are doing and track their achievement. Such visual displays give students, teachers, and parents very powerful ways to see the progress of a student's learning (Jackson and Lambert, 2013). Remember, the ultimate goal is reaching all the students in your classroom.

Some reluctant learners may have difficulty *remembering* basic math and science facts. Let us start with math. Remembering simple math combinations, even basic facts such as addition, subtraction, multiplication, and division, is difficult for many. There is no reason to be alarmed—strategies to improve recall skills can be taught.

Repetition games such as having the teacher call out a fact combination problem like "$4 \times 3 = \_\_$" and asking students to solve it, and then repeating with a new combination (such as "$2 \times 7 = \_\_$"), is one example. The game continues as each player calls out a new fact and each student responds with an answer. Students' ability to organize their thinking and use it to recall basic combinations will affect their success.

Quite often struggling students also have *attention* problems. They have trouble sustaining attention, avoiding distractions, and controlling their impulses. Some reluctant learners are easily distracted and have difficulty focusing on complex problems. It helps many students if the teacher arranges a structured, consistent classroom where clear expectations are carefully spelled out.

Although clear expectations can help, it is important to have space available for creative and critical thinking. It is not always necessary to tell students *how* to do a task. Let them come up with new ideas in different ways and monitor their progress.

Structure is often useful, but too much can stifle the imagination. Sometimes, it is best to supply the possibilities and let students decide how to reach various objectives.

> *Don't tell people how to do something. Tell them what to do and let them surprise you with their ingenuity.*
>
> —Anonymous

Effective use of visuals, manipulatives, and learning aids often help overcome various problems. Working in pairs or small groups is a good motivator. Peer involvement expands and strengthens language skills and increases students' confidence.

Struggling students with attention difficulties often have trouble with *time management* and changes between subjects and classes. They may also benefit from opportunities to be physically engaged in learning. Giving students many chances to move and interact with peers in structured situations is one of the keys to success.

Language problems can result in a bad attitude toward math and science. Even students whose first language is English are often confused by the vocabulary of these subjects. Words that have special meanings, such as "equals," "divisor," "sum," "cycle," or "properties," often slow down students' ability to focus and understand the terms being used.

When students fail to see the connections among concepts, math and science become a rote exercise, and understanding is limited. As experienced teachers will tell you, simply memorizing terms without knowing what they mean is not useful. Comprehension is the goal.

Student language understanding is helped by discussing important vocabulary, using creative writing strategies, and asking pertinent questions. Student learning is also assisted by reviewing previous concepts and demonstrating connections in problem-solving situations.

Metacognition is the ability to think about thinking. Students need to reflect on their own thinking in order to be aware of what they need to know (self-knowledge) and how they can go about acquiring information (procedural knowledge). As students become better at figuring out their own reasoning, they can also observe their own learning. This process includes evaluating whether they are learning, using helpful strategies when needed, and making changes when necessary.

As children grow and develop, they become better at thinking about their own thinking and how they think. This helps them move beyond their own personal perspective and better understand how others might think about a topic. These are critical skills for a math or science problem-solving situation.

Many struggling students do not understand that being successful in math and science involves employing problem-solving strategies. Teachers have to teach them how to be metacognitive learners and help them recognize the thinking strategies they are using. Metacognition strategies can amplify self-reliance and creativity for struggling learners. Teachers who model thought-fulness and encourage students to share problem-solving strategies with each other can go a long way toward fully engaging struggling students.

Students with a vast array of special needs are now found in the regular classroom (inclusion). In addition, the levels of language and cultural differences represented in elementary and middle schools continue to grow. The result is that today's classrooms include students with a very broad range of learning needs (Tucker et al., 2006).

A typical classroom today may include struggling students such as José, Maria, Jason, and Carlos. José struggles with a language-based learning problem. Maria has attention difficulties. Jason's inadequate reading skills interfere with his learning in all areas. And although Carlos has excellent cognitive abilities, he still has difficulty with math and science.

Whatever the reason for poor performance, youngsters need opportunities to learn about their individual strengths and weaknesses. The successful teaching of struggling students is most likely when teachers utilize culturally relevant materials, use collaborative instructional activities, and recognize that learning can take many forms through many modalities.

There are many ways to go about using collaborative activities in ways that build on the natural learning dispositions of a wide variety of cultural groups. Engaging in problem-solving strategies that are similar to those used in real-life situations certainly helps. And yes, celebrating individuality and working together to build successful learning communities certainly comple-ment each other.

COLLABORATIVE INQUIRY IN MATH AND SCIENCE

All students can flourish when good teaching is combined with collaborative inquiry and an engaging curriculum (Tomlinson and Imbeau, 2010). Collabo-rative inquiry is a form of reasoning and peer cooperation that begins with a problem and ends with a solution. It generally involves asking questions, observing, examining information, investigating, arriving at answers, and communicating the results.

A collaborative inquiry approach to the teaching of math and science has been found to work well with struggling learners. Among other things, it helps these students experience the excitement of mathematics and science activities in learning groups.

Knowledge of math and science has always been constructed in association with others. At all levels, mathematical and scientific inquiry is much more than an individual endeavor. So it is best if elementary and middle-school students employ procedures similar to the collaborative procedures that mathematicians and scientists actually use when they work.

The collaborative inquiry approach is a student-centered process of cooperative discovery. The teacher often gives the students directions and materials—but does not tell the small group exactly how to go about doing their work. The teacher encourages conversation and provides activities that help students understand how math and science are applied in the world outside of school. The teacher might also give a brief whole-class presentation and then move from small group to small group, encouraging questions and guiding student observations.

As students interact with materials and their peers, they can interact with math-science problems and jointly recognize the results of their investigation. The next step is applying what has been learned and recognizing that the knowledge acquired through inquiry is subject to change.

Learners certainly have different talents and interests, but they should all have access to high-quality math and science instruction. All students can be motivated with concrete materials, differentiated instruction, and cooperative experiences. But all these resources are especially important for students who are struggling with basic math and science concepts and skills.

Since student motivation is a major concern, it is important go beyond rote skill building to challenge reluctant learners. This means helping them deal with interesting, difficult, and ambiguous problems in which they are expected to discuss, question, and resolve problems themselves.

COLLABORATION, INQUIRY, AND RELUCTANT LEARNERS

Inquiry is sometimes thought of as the way people study the world and propose explanations based on the evidence they have accumulated. It involves actively seeking information, truth, and knowledge. When collaboration is added to the process, it helps build the positive relationships that are at the heart of a learning community.

Collaborative inquiry may be thought of as a range of concepts and techniques for enhancing interactive questioning, investigation, and learning. When questions that connect to student experiences are raised collectively, ideas and strengths are shared in a manner that supports the struggling students' search for understanding (Snow, 2005).

Teachers have found that using a collaborative approach to connect math and science instruction is a way to involve disinterested students in active small-group learning. When students work together as a team, they tend to motivate each other. Accomplishing shared goals benefits all of the individuals in a group and makes it more likely that collaboration will become a natural part of the fabric of instruction. The teacher provides a high degree of structure in forming groups and defining procedure, but students control the interactions within their groups. Building team-based organizational structures in the classroom makes it easier for teachers to reach out to students who have problems and ensure that all students are successful.

A shift in values and attitudes may be required for a collaborative learning environment to reach its full potential. Some traditional school environments have conditioned students to rely on the teacher to validate their thinking and direct learning. So getting over years of learned helplessness takes time. As they share and cooperate rather than compete for recognition, many children find more time for reflection and assessment. Although collaborative learning helps teachers achieve a number of motivational and social objectives, it also aims to improve student performance on academic tasks.

By tapping into students' social nature and natural curiosity, collaborative inquiry can go a long way toward helping struggling schools achieve academic and social goals. It is a disciplined and imaginative way of exploring and coming together in community with others. As they work in pairs or in small mixed-ability groups, students can take more responsibility for helping themselves and others learn. As teachers learn when and how to structure group lessons, collaboration can become a regular part of the day-to-day instructional program.

A Sample Collaborative Activity

This science and math example is designed to help students discover the diversity of seeds by using the process skills of predicting, comparing, categorizing, collecting data, organizing, recording, interpreting, and communicating. It is a collaborative inquiry activity that sets out to examine the tremendous diversity of plants and their seeds.

Math and Science Standards

- Math and science as inquiry—use appropriate tools to gather, organize, and interpret data.
- Think critically and logically to classify data and make connections between categories.

Materials: Science/math journal, brown paper bag, and pencil

Objectives

1. Students will work collaboratively.
2. Students will make predictions (guesses) about where the seed might be categorized.
3. Students will describe the categories verbally and in writing and the reasons for putting the seeds in them.
4. Students will classify seeds and describe the properties of seeds.
5. Students will compare and order their seeds.

Procedures

1. Introduce the concept of the great variety in plant seeds. Tell students that they are going to go on a seed hunt with a small group of two or three other classmates. Their task is to try to find and collect samples of one seed for each of the following categories: seeds that float, seeds that blow, seeds that hitchhike, helicopter seeds, seeds that twirl, and seeds that are cycled through animals or need animals to grow.
2. Instruct students to record where the seed was located in their math/ science journals. Students may wish to describe, draw, or write their feelings about finding the seeds.
3. Upon returning, students will be asked to guess where the seed may be categorized. Encourage them to write their predictions in their journals.

Evaluation

1. Have student groups bring their seeds back to the class to compare their findings and test their predictions with other groups.
2. Have students divide and save the seeds in their portfolios.

3. Have students reflect on this activity.

Reflections

1. Allow students time to discuss and write their reflections.
2. Students may wish to imagine they are the seeds their group collected and compare themselves to their seeds.
3. Ask students how the group felt about being seeds.
4. Ask students how this activity relates to their lives.

MAKING INSTRUCTIONAL DECISIONS WITH DIFFERENTIATED LEARNING

Because we know that students learn in different ways and at different rates, it is important to consider differentiating instruction. The basic idea is to provide individual students with different avenues for learning content. Differentiated learning is an organized approach through which teachers and students work together in planning, setting goals, and monitoring progress. In such classrooms, the teacher draws on the cultural knowledge of students by using culturally and personally relevant examples. They show respect for learners by valuing their similarities and differences, not by treating everybody the same.

Teachers are the main organizers, but students often help with the design. It is the teacher's job to know what is important and to analyze and offer the best approach to learning. Students can let teachers know when materials or assignments are too hard or too easy and when learning is interesting (or when it is not). As a collaborative effort in shaping all parts of the learning experience, students will assume ownership of their learning.

Understanding how students adapt to learning environments and classroom structure is crucial. When teachers focus on students' strengths, students become more interested and work to achieve. Learners who struggle are frequently rebellious and out of sorts in a learning environment that does not adequately address different teaching strategies and learning styles. This can result in failure for these students, starting with inaccurate diagnosis and remedial work, or sometimes even withdrawal from school.

The most useful teaching approach for the struggling learner is often well-organized differentiated instruction (Tomlinson and Cunningham Eidson, 2003). A teacher who is organized examines the conditions surrounding the child, such as curriculum content, the classroom environment, and the student's academic and social behaviors. The ways students react to information and respond to feedback are also important. Planning for manageable units of classroom time and including as many teaching and behavioral approaches as possible certainly help. But teachers know that no approach is effective in every situation, so it is important to be flexible. They also know that when they depend too much on rote memorization (devoid of meaningful applications), many students have trouble recognizing and retaining math/science facts and drawing conclusions.

In general, today's standards-driven curriculum provides many opportunities for students to develop a real understanding of mathematics and science content. As learners become more skillful and experienced, math and science ideas can be built upon and related to previous learning. Disaffected students, too often, are assigned uninteresting drill work each year to help them learn "basic skills." Yet we know that students who did not understand the concept the first time are not likely to "catch on" the next time. Limiting their chances for math and science reasoning and problem solving puts struggling students at a serious disadvantage (Karp and Howell, 2004). It does not take long for youngsters to get the message that teachers have low expectations when it comes to their academic achievement.

Achievement gaps often result when math and science content is not connected to students' ability levels and experiences. What conditions will foster improved achievement? Research has not provided many clear-cut answers. Some suggest student absences or movement between schools may account for some of the problems. Other factors include the child's developmental environment and the home and school learning conditions. Gaps exist not only in the curriculum but also between the student and some of the challenging content of math and science.

What works for reluctant learners? Among other things, working with peers can help disaffected students focus and feel good about themselves. Opportunities to communicate with others, as part of interesting math and science activities, can make also these subjects more motivating. Such a team-based approach is particularly powerful when student efforts are rewarded by peers and the teacher.

DISCOVERING WAYS TO DIFFERENTIATE INSTRUCTION

In a differentiated classroom, the teacher accepts students as they are and helps them succeed considering their unique circumstances. Differentiated classrooms are places where the teacher carefully designs instruction around the important concepts, principles, and skills of each subject. The helpful teacher makes sure that struggling learners focus on essential understandings and important skills. The subject is introduced in a way that each student finds meaningful and interesting. Although the teacher intends to have all students attain these skills, he or she knows that many will not achieve all there is to know (Tomlinson, 1999).

Recognizing individual learning styles and adapting a differentiated teaching style can make learning easier. With differentiated learning, the teacher provides specific ways for each student to learn deeply, working energetically to ensure that all students work harder than they imagined and achieve more than they thought possible (Tomlinson, 2001).

What is clear is that struggling students seem to have the hardest time with the traditional classroom setting (straight desks, teacher lectures, textbooks, worksheets, lots of listening, waiting, following directions, reading, and writing). In other environments, students who struggle have much less difficulty, for example, in an art classroom, a wood shop, a dance floor, or the outdoors. In these differentiated classroom settings where students have opportunities to engage in movement, hands-on learning, arts education, project-based learning, and other new learning approaches, their interest and desire to learn have been shown to be at or above average (Gardner, 1993).

There are ways that teachers can differentiate or modify instruction to guarantee that each student will learn as much and as competently as possible: Teachers can modify the content of what is taught and the ways in which they give students information. They can also help students understand the process of how they learn important knowledge and skills. Did they use manipulatives to aid in their understanding? Did they ask others? Teachers want to know what the student understands and is able to do. Did the student show his or her work? The teacher is also interested in discovering students' thoughts and feelings in the classroom. How did students react to the learning environment or the way the class atmosphere worked?

There are several student characteristics that teachers respond to as they design differentiated lessons. They include readiness (what a student knows, understands, and is able to do today), interest (what a student enjoys learning about), and learning profile (a student's preferred learning style).

Several Sample Strategies for Differentiating Instruction

Readiness

Provide books at different reading levels.
Use activities at various levels of difficulty but focused on the same
    learning goal.

Interest

Encourage students to use a variety of media arrangements such as video,
    music, film, and computers to express their ideas.
Use collaborative group work to explore topics of interest.

Learning Profile

Present a project in a visual, auditory, or movement style.
Develop activities that use many viewpoints on interesting topics and
    issues.

Today's classrooms are challenging environments for teachers. Designing lessons that are responsive to the individual needs of all students is not an easy task. Teaching math and science in a differentiated classroom can be challenging, especially when teachers are trying to increase the emphasis on math and science inquiry process skills. Skills such as communicating, observing, reasoning, measuring, making connections, experimenting, and problem solving are only a few of the processes of doing mathematics and science.

MEETING THE PRINCIPLES AND STANDARDS

The six principles discussed below describe important issues of the mathematics and science curriculum standards. Used together, the principles will come alive as teachers develop comprehensive school math and science programs.

- *Equity*: High-quality mathematics and science require raising expectations for students' learning. All students must have opportunities to study and learn mathematics and science. This does not mean that every student should receive identical instruction; instead, it demands that appropriate accommodations be made for all students. Resources and classroom support are also a large part of equity.

- *Curriculum*: A curriculum must be coherent, focused on math and science, and articulated across grade levels. Interconnected strands effectively organize and integrate mathematical and scientific ideas so that students can understand how one idea builds on and connects with other ideas. Building deeper understandings provides a map for guiding teachers through the different levels of learning.

- *Technology*: Technology today is an essential part of learning and understanding math and science. The effectiveness of mathematics and science teaching is dramatically increased with technological tools. Tools such as calculators and computers provide visual images of math and science ideas. They facilitate learning by organizing and analyzing data, and they compute accurately. Technology resources from the Internet to computer programs like Logo provide useful tools for mathematics and science learning.

- *Assessment*: Assessment should support the learning of math and science and provide useful information to students and teachers. This enhances students' learning while providing a valuable aid for making instructional teaching decisions.

- *Teaching*: Effective teachers understand mathematics and science, comprehend what underachieving students know and need to learn, and challenge and support them through learning experiences. Teachers need multiple kinds of knowledge: knowledge of the subject, pedagogical knowledge, and an understanding of how children learn. Different techniques and instructional materials also affect how well their students learn mathematics and science. Struggling learners are often inundated with only practice materials trying to help them master the "basic skills." They often lack the conceptual foundations of real understanding. Students frequently forget procedures and are referred back to the same uninteresting skill-based drill work. The learner is not the focus; rather, the basic skill drill is the center of attention.

- *Learning*: Math and science must be learned with understanding. Students actively build new knowledge from prior experience. Students should have the ability to use knowledge in a flexible manner, applying what is learned, and melding factual knowledge with conceptual understandings—thus making learning easier. The learning principle is used when all students are involved in authentic and challenging work. Struggling students' interest is sparked, and they create a strong understanding of the basic skills, regardless of whether it is through games, peer involvement, or simple quiz situations.

STRUGGLING LEARNERS AND THE MATH AND SCIENCE STANDARDS

The new millennium has ushered in extraordinary changes. In mathematics and science, new knowledge and new ways of learning, doing, and communicating continue to evolve. Today, inexpensive calculators are everywhere. Powerful media outlets widely disseminate information as mathematics and science continue to filter into our lives.

> *If students can't learn the way we teach, we must teach them the way they learn.*
>
> —Carol Ann Tomlinson

We want all students, particularly struggling learners, to be involved in high-quality engaging mathematics and science instruction. High expectations should be set for all, with accommodations for those who need them. As students become confident about engaging in math and science tasks, they learn to observe, explore evidence, and provide reasoning and proof to support their conclusions. As they become active and resourceful problem solvers, students learn to be flexible as they participate in learning groups (with access to technology).

Students value mathematics and science when they work productively and reflectively—communicating their ideas orally and in writing (NCTM, 2000; NRC, 1996). This is not a just highly ambitious dream but also a successful effort to influence instruction. Here we reference some of the principles behind the new standards and offer suggestions for effective teaching.

The National Council of Teachers of Mathematics and the National Science Foundation have developed standards that serve as guides for focused and enduring efforts to improve students' school mathematics and science education. These content standards provide a comprehensive set of standards for teaching mathematics and science from kindergarten through grade 12.

An Overview of the Curriculum and Evaluation Standards for School Mathematics

The principles and standards for school mathematics recommend that all students

- understand numbers and operations and estimate and use computational tools effectively.
- understand and use various patterns and relationships.
- use problem solving to explore and understand mathematical content.
- analyze geometric characteristics and use visualization and spatial reasoning to solve problems within and outside mathematics.
- pose questions, collect, organize, represent, and interpret data to evaluate arguments.
- apply basic notions of chance and probability.
- understand and use attributes, units, and systems of measurement and apply a variety of techniques and tools for determining measurements.
- recognize reasoning and proof as essential to mathematics.
- use mathematical thinking to communicate ideas clearly.
- create and use representations to model, organize, record, and interpret mathematical ideas.

(These are brief selections. For a full description, see NCTM, 2000.)

An Overview of the National Science Education Standards

Principles that guide the standards:

- Science is for all students.
- Learning is an active process.
- School science reflects the intellectual and cultural traditions that characterize the practice of contemporary science.
- Improving science education is part of a systemic educational reform.

The science standards highlight what students should know, understand, and be able to do. Examples include the following:

- Becoming aware of physical, life, earth, and space sciences through activity-based learning.
- Connecting the concepts and processes in science.

- Using science as inquiry.
- Understanding the relationship between science and technology.
- Using science understandings to design solutions to problems.
- Identifying with the history and nature of science through readings, discussions, observations, and written communications.
- Viewing and practicing science using personal and social perspectives. (National Academy Press, 1996)

As far as the subjects of math, science, and technology are concerned, even the experts often have no idea of future directions. Oddly enough, the ambiguity of what is going to come next meshes with the spirit of scientific inquiry, technological innovation, and mathematical problem solving.

GOING BEYOND SKILL MASTERY

Students who complete their math and science lessons with little understanding quickly forget or confuse the procedures. For example, in doing a long division problem, suppose that students cannot recall if they are supposed to divide the numerator into the denominator, or the reverse, in order to find the correct decimal. They can do the problem either way, but they may not understand what they are doing or be able to explain their reasoning.

Understanding and skill mastery go together when students build on ideas they already know in a discovery process. In science, step-by-step directions for an experiment often are quickly given and extra time is not provided for explanation. Again, the goal should be to understand what is going on well enough to know how it can be applied in the world outside school.

Understanding important ideas and accurately completing problems are some of the first steps in becoming mathematically and scientifically skillful. Mathematics and science learning contains five strands of thought:

1. Understanding ideas and being able to comprehend important content.
2. Being flexible and using accurate procedures.
3. Posing and solving problems.
4. Reflecting and evaluating knowledge.
5. Reasoning and making sense and value out of what is learned.

Oftentimes, the struggling student has experienced little success in the five strands. Math and science success can be expected and achieved as adaptations are made to the students' curriculum. This can happen when teachers relate problems to real-life student interests and provide time for collaborative work.

Organizing Successful Lessons

Students reach higher rates of proficiency when they are involved in organized lessons that pay special attention to their individual learning needs.

Stage 1: Review

Students connect new math and science concepts to old ideas they are familiar with when they are actively engaged at a concrete level of understanding. Math and science manipulatives such as counters, eye droppers, rulers, and blocks are used to answer questions that represent interesting real-life problems. For example, students are asked to show how many more cupcakes need to be made for a class picnic if seven are already made for the class of sixteen students (each student gets one cupcake). Connections are made to former lessons, such as relating subtraction to the mathematical idea of how many more. Questions are asked, and students discuss their understanding of the mathematical ideas.

Stage 2: Demonstrate Knowledge or Skill

Next, students show their thinking by drawing a picture of the problem. For example, the set of cupcakes might be shown like this: "I have 7 cupcakes. How many more do we need to get 16?" Have students draw a basket to show their results.

Stage 3: Guided Practice

Students form a number sentence to match their drawings. $7 + \_\_ = 16$. (Answer: 9). We needed 9 more than 7 to get 16. Students fill in numerals and number sentences.

Stage 4: Check for Understanding

In the last part of the lesson, students practice skills and problems through a range of activities and supporting lessons. The teacher provides ongoing feedback at each step so that procedural errors can be corrected.

Organized Strategies to Support Students with Learning Problems

1. Review important concepts—make connections between familiar and new information.
2. Demonstrate knowledge or skill—increase student engagement and promote independent student activities.
3. Provide guided practice—reinforce language skills, partner, and share. Students do a variety of problems.
4. Check for understanding and provide feedback—summarize strategies and evaluate.
5. Teacher provides continuous reinforcement at each stage so that errors can be found and corrected.

Assessing Students' Strengths

Math and science content knowledge, student learning styles, behaviors, and reinforcement that affect learning are all considered in assessment. Assessment data is gathered from teacher observations, performance on daily assignments, math and science quizzes, homework, and in-class work. This information is recorded on a student data sheet. The value of assessment is that it leads to an overall analysis of a student's strengths and weaknesses.

Student Data Sheet

1. Learning setting—indicates the physical environment in which the student works.
2. Content—includes the subject matter in which the child is engaged.
3. Process—involves strategies, methods, and tools that students are engaged in (e.g., listening and speaking).
4. Behavior—refers to academic and social behaviors that students demonstrate.
5. Reinforcement—looks at responses from the learning environment that cause behaviors to occur.

Recording Behavior Patterns

Behaviors that are consistent are called likely behaviors. They might include the desire to play video games or use the computer. Unlikely behaviors describe behaviors that usually occur below an average rate or at a very minimal level. For example, a classroom environment that is conducive to student achievement could be rated with a "1" symbol. If a student is having problems in the classroom environment, the teacher would mark this category with a "2" symbol. Collecting and reviewing this information with students allow teachers to focus on recognizing which classroom activities foster positive behaviors.

Creating Math and Science Success Plans

Math and science instruction focuses on student learning while building on students' strengths and identifying error patterns. The teacher judges the students' data sheets, recording the type of learning environment that students were involved in. The content of the lessons is also recorded. The learners' preferred learning style and how they accept and express themselves (including listening, speaking, writing, or drawing) are also recorded information.

The teacher notes if the student works well with others or works best alone. The students' academic and social participation are other factors considered when evaluating the students' data sheets. Learners' responses are documented. Examples of learner responses that are recorded include "likes being with friends," "enjoys helping in class," "likes being in front of class," "does not turn in work on time," "cannot stay focused," or "talks out of turn."

Based on identifying how students learn, the Sample Math and Science Success Plan is designed to recognize and move students toward more positive behaviors and academic success. In this way, the Sample Math and Science Success Plan serves as a guide for an organized and well-planned learning approach for struggling learners.

Instruction now tends to be more research based and standards driven. It often involves learners constructing deeper content knowledge through collaborative inquiry. Modern math and science learning is much more than memorizing a collection of isolated rules and procedures. Understanding and application involve certain levels of reasoning, problem solving, and imagination. Chance and uncertainty play major roles along the path to developing cultures of intellectual curiosity and innovation.

Time	30 minutes	15-20 minutes	20-30 minutes
Context	One on one with teacher Small-group setting	With peers With teacher	Working independently
Content	Specific activities	Groups objects in 10s	Records quantities
Process	Counts aloud Oral instructions	Oral activities	Reports answers orally
Behavior	Completes assignments Works carefully	Turns in assignments Accepts teacher directions Positive response	Monitoring for student use of self-control
Reinforcement	Oral feedback Allowed movement in classroom		Group activities Peer work

Sample Math and Science Success Plan

There are, after all, multiple ways of charting the way forward—and very different ways to successfully go about solving problems. So it is little wonder that so many of us have trouble dealing with the arbitrary nature of individual and societal destiny.

Building Creative Understanding and Academic Success

Creativity, originality, and exploring future possibilities are often a matter of perspective. Sometimes it involves digging up new ground—and sometimes it is going over old ground differently.

Recognizing the learning characteristics of all students and finding instructional methods that motivate them are important steps in math and science instruction. The basic idea is to use strategies that consider all aspects of the learners' instructional needs so that they can use their imaginations and be successful.

The instructional methods mobilized for reluctant learners must not get in the way of the students who are already doing well in math and science. Differentiated learning and collaboration help reach the unmotivated, while providing meaningful opportunities for everyone in the classroom (Hehir and Katzman, 2013).

Math and science certainly do not attract universal affection. In fact, anything even faintly mathematical or scientific engenders fear in many. Such an attitude has long been referred to as an "American phobia" (Burns, 1998). Still, regardless of whether they know it, all individuals use and are affected by math and science in their day-to-day lives. In many respects, these disciplines cannot be avoided.

In order to do well in any subject, students need to have a fairly positive—or at least disciplined—attitude toward achieving mastery. Also, both students and teachers may have to be willing to adapt and change to maximize learning.

The educational process involves much more than what happens at school. One way or another, everyone is involved in the education of children and young adults. So when it comes to who is to blame for educational problems, it goes well beyond the classroom door.

Educators need to be aware of how social forces (including the family) influence what is learned in the classroom. This does not mean that parents have to teach math and science outside of school, although that would not hurt. It is just that the home and social environment matter when it comes to learning.

The self-esteem and spirit of individuals and groups are often expressed through culture. All students are helped when community resources, issues, events, and topics connect to what happens in the classroom (Van de Walle and Lovin, 2006).

Past and present experiences outside of school can serve as powerful resources for learning. In addition, purposeful classroom linkages with the home environment can be created and sustained by the math/science curricula and by the actions of the teacher. There are even situations, especially at the early childhood level, in which parents may have to be coached and rewarded for becoming better caregivers.

As teachers use an organized approach to assess their students' math/science strengths (and error patterns), they can put into practice learning strategies that connect a student's predisposition to a positive classroom-learning environment. One of the things that helps is having students explore the practical applications of math and science in their lives.

Math/science rules need to be connected to student understandings in a way that offers them an authentic invitation to interesting problems. This organized approach may well be the best way to get struggling students to express their reasoning in ways that can lead to academic success (Muschla et al., 2012). While opening doors to understanding for reluctant learners, teachers must not slow down those who are already motivated and doing well.

Getting young people to work as part of a team is one thing, but getting them to appreciate math and science can be more difficult. Experienced teachers know a lot about making the classroom a positive experience. They also know that for many disaffected students, it helps if they can work with others.

Effective teachers frequently use interactive mixed-ability group strategies as they adapt techniques from a wide repertoire of methods.

Since it is best to use all the tools available, technologies like the Internet can prove useful when it comes to encouraging collaborative inquiry and learning by doing. For example, some teachers like students to work in pairs as they write on classroom wikis and websites (editing each other's writing is part of the process).

SUMMARY, CONCLUSION, AND LOOKING AHEAD

Mathematics and technology are tools of science *and* they are subjects in their own right. All three topics influence and feed off of each other. Thriving in an innovation-driven world requires generating high-quality learning experiences at the earliest possible level.

It is difficult to overstate the impact of the technological products of math and science. A good example is the set of virtual global connections and social structures that are changing how we think, live, and work. It is important for young people to develop the ability to mitigate the potential risks as technology pushes out to new frontiers.

As students grow and master more advanced skills they will interpret their experiences through many of the patterns of ideas, values, and beliefs that they learned early on.

At every age level, it is important to think big and risk failure to make new ideas and positive change possible. It does not all have to happen at once—teachers can think big and start small as they weave new ideas into the educational fabric.

As a larger proportion of the population is able to meet higher educational standards, it is bound to lead to more innovation, higher incomes, and a more productive economy. It does not take a university degree to be successful and make a social contribution. But everyone *does* need to have at least some post-secondary training. (Take a look at how Germany conducts its apprenticeship programs.)

In an innovation-driven changing world, we may never fully succeed in providing exactly the same opportunities for everyone. But we can do better, much better, by providing high-quality instruction for all students—especially unmotivated learners and others who may be struggling to master math or science content.

When bringing technology into the math/science classroom, it is best to build on what you already do well. At the K–8 level, that probably means small collaborative groups and student activities or projects.

Humans are not designed to get their basic understanding about subjects by sitting alone in front of a computer or video screen. Although online education has gotten off to a rocky start, hybrid courses that include a mix of face-to-face learning and online work show some promise.

At least a fair amount of offline social interaction is needed for imaginative new ideas and innovation to fully flower. There are, after all, many situations in which academic success requires face-to-face problem-solving activities in combination with online experiences or virtual reality simulations in order for active learning to reach its full potential.

Even in a technology-rich classroom environment, creativity and innovation are processes that are sometimes difficult for the teacher to get across to their students. However, building on the social nature of learning (in which everyone involved comes together) makes it possible to improve the odds.

The most important and innovative applications of math, science, and technology involve communities, networks, institutions, and changing social attitudes. With or without technology, overall educational success has a lot to do with the level of support in the surrounding culture.

Improving student outcomes is most likely to happen at the intersection of individual imaginative processes and the collaboration associated with generating new ideas.

Numerous aspects of good teaching exist in a gray zone where there are no black and white answers. Educational research and the content standards matter, but an overreaching reliance on experts and nebulous metrics can get in the way of positive change. Many things that can be counted or measured do not matter all that much. And many of the things that matter cannot be counted.

The process of teacher evaluation and improvement has to be built on what teachers actually do and how their students learn (Darling-Hammond, 2013). For a teacher to grow and change in a way that enriches what goes on in the classroom requires combining professional development with participation in the professional community. Within schools, collegial help and activity have to go hand in hand with mutual respect and support.

When it comes to student learning, there is no substitute for a good teacher who develops lessons that combine thinking and feeling in a way that reaches both the head and the heart.

Clearly, a student's academic success is strongly influenced by the teacher's energy, knowledge, character, sense of humor, and ability to relate to young people. If we want all students to master math and science, there has to be a highly skilled teacher in every classroom.

> *Major changes in the productivity of American schools rest on our ability to create and sustain a highly prepared teaching force for all, not just some, of our children.*
>
> —Linda Darling-Hammond

QUESTIONS FOR TEACHERS AND PROSPECTIVE TEACHERS

1. Interview four peers. Ask them if they ever had difficulty learning math and science. Have them identify their reasons and explain.
2. How would you identify a struggling learner and include him in small-group work?
3. What are some teaching ideas for connecting math and science to students' needs and interests?
4. Are digital technologies barging into the classroom before we have the ability to understand their implications or possibilities?
5. How does learning mathematics and science today differ from how you were taught? Provide examples.

REFERENCES AND RESOURCES

Armstrong, T. (2012). *Neurodiversity in the Classroom: Strength-based Strategies to Help Students with Special Needs to Succeed in School and Life.* Alexandria, VA: Association for Supervision and Curriculum Development.

Burns, M. (1998). *Math: Facing an American Phobia.* White Plains, NY: Math Solutions Publications.

Common Core State Standards Initiative. (2013). "Mathematics Standards." Available online at http://www.corestandards.org/Math.

Darling-Hammond, L. (2013). *Getting Teacher Evaluation Right: What Matters for Effectiveness and Improvement.* New York, NY: Teachers College Press.

Dudley-Marling, C., ed. (2012). *High-Expectation Curricula: Helping Students Succeed with Powerful Learning.* New York, NY: Teachers College Press.

Elmore, R. (2004). *School Reform from the Inside Out: Policy, Practice, and Performance.* Cambridge, MA: Harvard University Press.

Gardner, H. (1993). *Multiple Intelligences: The Theory in Practice.* New York, NY: Basic Books.

Hehir, T., & Katzman, L. (2013). *Effective Schools: Designing Effective Schoolwide Programs.* San Francisco, CA: Jossey-Bass.

Karp, K., & Howell, P. (2004). Building Responsibility for Learning in Students with Special Needs. *Teaching Children Mathematics* 11 (3): 118–126.

Kirp, D. (2013). *Improbable Scholars. The Rebirth of a Great American School System and a Strategy for American Schools.* Oxford, UK: Oxford University Press.

Jackson, R., & Lambert, C. (2013). *How to Support Struggling Students.* Alexandria, VA: Association for Supervision and Curriculum Development.

Mayer-Schonberger, V., & Cukier, K. (2013). *Big Data: A Revolution that Will Transform How We Live, Work, and Think.* Geneva, IL: Eamon Dolan/Houghton Mifflin Harcourt.

Muschla, J. A., Muschla, G. R., & Muschla, E. (2012). *Teaching the Common Core Math Standards with Hands-On Activities, Grades 6–8.* San Francisco, CA: Jossey-Bass.

Musser, G. L., Burger, W. F., & Peterson, B. E. (2005). *Mathematics for Elementary Teachers: A Contemporary Approach.* Hoboken, NJ: John Wiley & Sons.

National Academy Press. (1996). *National Science Education Standards.* Washington, DC: National Academy Press.

National Council of Teachers of Mathematics (NCTM). (2000). *Principles and Standards for School Mathematics.* Reston, VA: National Council of Teachers of Mathematics.

National Research Council (NRC). (1996). *National Science Education Standards.* Washington, DC: National Academy Press.

National Research Council. (2001). *Everybody Counts: A Report to the Nation on the Future of Mathematics Education.* Washington, DC: National Research Council.

Peters, J. M., & Stout, D. L. (2005). *Science in Elementary Education: Methoconcepts and Inquiries.* Upper Saddle, NJ: Prentice Hall.

Polya, G. (2004). *How to Solve It: A New Aspect of Mathematical Method.* Princeton, NJ: Princeton University Press.

Safro, J. (2005). *Math Word Problems Made Easy: Grade 5.* Woodhills, CA: Scholastic Teaching Resources.

Sherman, H., Richardson, L., & Yard, G. (2009). *Teaching Learners Who Struggle with Mathematics: Systematic Intervention and Remediation.* Upper Saddle River, NJ: Pearson Education, Inc.

Small, M. (2012). *Eyes on Math: A Visual Approach to Teaching Math Concepts.* New York, NY: Teachers College Press.

Snow, D. (2005). *Classroom Strategies for Helping At-Risk Students.* Aurora, CO: Mid-continent Research for Education and Learning.

Tomlinson, C. (1999). *The Differentiated Classroom: Responding to the Needs of All Learners.* Alexandria, VA: Association for Supervision and Curriculum Development.

Tomlinson, C. (2001). *How to Differentiate Instruction in Mixed-Ability Classrooms.* 2nd ed. Alexandria, VA: Association for the Supervision and Curriculum Development.

Tomlinson, C., & Cunningham Eidson, C. (2003). *Differentiation in Practice: A Resource Guide for Differentiating Curriculum.* Alexandria, VA: Association for Supervision and Curriculum Development.

Tomlinson, C. A., & Imbeau, M. B. (2010). *Leading and Managing a Differentiated Classroom.* Alexandria, VA: Association for Supervision & Curriculum Development.

Tucker, B., Singleton, A., & Weaver, T. (2006). *Teaching Mathematics to ALL Children: Designing and Adapting Instruction to Meet the Needs of Diverse Learners.* 2nd ed. Upper Saddle River, NJ: Prentice Hall.

Van de Walle, J., & Lovin, L., (2006). *Teaching Student-centered Mathematics.* Boston, MA: Pearson/Allyn & Bacon.

Chapter Two

Creative and Inventive Thinking

*Collaborative Inquiry, Open-Ended Problem
Solving, and Innovation*

*Imagination is the beginning of creation
You imagine what you desire
You will what you imagine
You create what you will*

—George Bernard Shaw

Innovation is a place where thinking meets up with problems to do new things and do old things in new ways. It has a lot to do with developing ideas that extend inventive thinking in a way that goes beyond standard models. At school or in the workplace, success has a lot to do with teamwork and the quality of the group.

Imaginative problem solving, technology-related applications, and collaborative inquiry have important roles to play in creating tomorrow's innovators.

Creative and innovative thinking are included in any recipe for coming up with unique ideas that have value. Another ingredient is the ability to generate original ideas and imaginative responses to problems or situations. Creative expression in a world of constant flux builds on original self-expression, reasoned insights, and communication.

Critical thinking may be thought of as an intellectually disciplined way of actively and skillfully conceptualizing, analyzing, synthesizing, and applying information. Definitions vary, but here academic thinking skills are viewed

31

as the mental processes that are needed to organize, understand, and apply certain principles of complex subjects like math, science, and technology.

Different types of thinking and imaginative processes frequently overlap and reinforce one another. The human mind has a natural ability to figure out what kind of creativity and thought processes are needed to solve a particular problem. But whatever the mix of reasoning skills, the development of powerful new ideas has a lot to do with being able to challenge the conventional approaches to making sense of the world.

When it comes to promoting more thoughtful work in the classroom, it makes sense for the teacher to encourage students to ask questions, investigate, and use evidence to come up with imaginative solutions. It is also up to the teacher to create opportunities for students to make connections between concepts and come up with imaginative approaches for solving problems.

THOUGHTFUL PROBLEM SOLVING AND INQUIRY

Problem solving is at the heart of mathematics; *inquiry* is equally important to science education. Both are compatible with developing highly refined reasoning skills. And both subjects are more likely to thrive when differentiated learning is used as an instructional framework for encouraging creativity and innovative ideas in the classroom.

With differentiated learning, the teacher tailors lessons to meet individual needs and interests. Differentiated instruction (DI) is an approach that can help teachers figure out *how* to teach. Subject matter standards are more likely to suggest *what* should be taught.

DI involves making subjects more accessible to every student in the classroom. It builds on the fact that learners have different views, perspectives, preferences, and strengths that must be taken into account.

When teachers combine opportunities for choice and discovery with thoughtful risk taking, the result is often the bubbling up of innovative energy and imaginative activity. The basic idea is that if we can imagine it and gather the strength of will to sustain it, then we can create it.

Creative and innovative thinking are important skills needed to meet the challenges of living and succeeding in the twenty-first century (Robinson, 2011).

These skills should be near the center of education; they amplify enthusiasm for learning and generate new solutions for the most pressing problems of today and tomorrow.

An education that ignores new realities and imaginative approaches is incomplete. Viewing math, science, and technology as creative subjects amplifies subject matter competency, thinking skills, and innovative tendencies.

Creative and innovative thinking is now such an important part of analytical problem solving in math and collaborative inquiry in science that it cannot be ignored. As the content standards and Common Core suggest, the worth of the ideas created has a lot to do with how the problem being explored is defined.

The Common Core State Standards are a set of learner goals laid out by grade level and subject. Take the example of mathematics: The aim is to get teachers and students to be more thoughtful and analytical. Most states are involved, and student progress is measured by tests that go well beyond multiple-choice questions.

Both the new Common Core and the influential subject matter standards pay close attention to developing creative talent. Along with content, emphasis is on thinking, not telling students what to think. Collaborative inquiry and problem solving are viewed as going hand in hand with intellectual curiosity and open-minded persistence.

The activities that you will find in this book are standards driven and research based. They are designed to help students open new doors to thinking and learning possibilities in math, science, and technology. All along the path to student understanding, teachers need to pay close attention to learning targets and explain them to students.

Student goal setting, self-assessment, and higher-order thinking skills can be helped along by differentiating instructional content (Moss and Brookhart, 2012). As teachers design lessons, they must consider a student's readiness, interests, learning profile, and teamwork skills.

Effective teachers know that it is possible to respond to differing needs even when students are working with a partner or in small groups. This is especially true if lessons are designed so that they are meaningful for every individual. Also, the creative and critical imagination is amplified through appealing to different interests in a community of responsible and reflective learners.

Teachers who choose to differentiate lessons begin where students are and build on the belief that students learn in quite different ways. The basic idea is that varying the speed and complexity of instruction helps each individual reason and learn as deeply and as efficiently as possible.

To increase student motivation, teachers often encourage students to put thinking skills to work in analyzing and solving problems that are part of the world within which they live. Whether it is in or out of school, innovation does not occur in a vacuum; rather, it draws on the ability to acquire knowledge and apply it in new situations.

Annoying speed bumps are one of the costs of innovation. At any age, innovators must trust themselves to push through roadblocks to achieve their vision; at the same time, they must balance being open to new ideas and continual self- and peer assessment. Throughout the process of identifying needs, asking good questions, and trying out new ideas, self-confidence without sufficient questioning is a recipe for disaster.

Nurturing the idea that twenty-first-century innovation involves risk and effort is part of helping students come up with fresh answers to the questions posed and the data collected. Teachers can promote creativity by making collaboration a normal part of the daily routine and encouraging students to express themselves using multiple media.

The fact that basic skills of one generation may prove inadequate for the next makes it difficult for teachers, parents, communities, and the students themselves. Many factors that influence thinking are generated far from the educational and family worlds.

Popular culture may be an oxymoron, but children who grow up in a nonlinear world of television, computers, iPads, video games, and related Internet associates may have an advantage over adults in adapting to the chaotic world of technological change.

Will the future place a higher value on the length of a person's attention span or on the ability to do many things at the same time? With a multitasking tidal wave crashing over today's youngsters, it seems unlikely they will be as able as their elders when it comes to sustaining the more linear aspects of thoughtful inquiry. However this all gets sorted out, you can be sure that creativity and innovation will be part of the basic skill fabric needed for success in the world of tomorrow.

In a rapidly changing, innovation-driven world, economic development comes from new techniques and processes that are fueled by the imagination. As Americans discovered after World War II, big investments in innovation, research, and education (human capital) led to the dissemination and commercialization of new ideas. Why turn stingy many decades later?

Math, science, technology, and fresh ideas are, more than ever, the keys to a productive future. Another thing that has not changed in the twenty-first century is that a nation's growth and prosperity depend on some combination of natural resources, ideas, and innovation.

The Societal Impact on Creative and Critical Thinking

Thinking skills, particularly those related to innovation, extend over time and have a lot to do with originality, adaptability, and accomplishment. New curriculum standards and teaching methods pay closer attention now more than ever to problem solving and inquiry related to the world outside of school.

One of the ways of doing this is by encouraging student thought processes that are similar to those used by mathematicians, scientists, and technology experts as they go about designing real-world applications. The basic approach is to collect data, select information, and reflect on what it might mean for the natural world.

Developing a deep understanding of a subject or process naturally leads to application. Along the way, it is important that neither science nor its mathematical and technological tools be separated from humanism. And remember, many people are systematically too confident. For example, there is often a tendency to put too much weight on information you like and too little on data that contradicts your assumptions.

Often breakthroughs come from those who are well prepared in fields that are different from those where the discovery takes place. But whether it is a professional from another field or an amateur, the results are usually best when there is some kind of interaction with professionals knowledgeable about the subject.

As students develop critical thinking skills, it becomes more natural to approach a task in a realistic way, while leaving room for unconventional, spontaneous, flexible, and original ideas. Sometimes this is done within a preexisting paradigm, and at other times it means breaking out of conventional boundaries.

Creative and innovative thinking are constructed by the mind and strongly influenced by personal experience. Various attributes of thoughtfulness (like intelligence, personality, and values) can naturally develop along with math, science, and technology skills. Science, for example, teaches respect for evidence, doubt, and opposing points of view. The quality of an individual's thinking is also influenced by their personal, academic, and cultural background.

Various elements of thoughtfulness develop along with other attributes of functional intelligence and personality. Using math, science, and related technological tools forces us to change ourselves by making us think and rethink what we know. As students go about this process, they grow better at reasoning inductively and deductively across the curriculum (McIntosh and Warren, 2013).

Being good at thinking means being able to form alternative explanations and demonstrate intellectual curiosity in a manner that is flexible, elaborate, and novel to the thinker. As part of their responsibility to the future, teachers must respect the unique ideas developed by children and encourage the development of thinking skills. It seems clear that many future problems will be solved by people who are flexible, open, original, and creatively productive.

Good creative and innovative thinking activities encourage students to analyze underlying assumptions that influence meanings and interpretations of information. Such intellectually demanding thinking leads children to identify, clarify, and solve problems and become more innovative.

The questions explored can be as general as "Are there limits to how much of the physical universe we can understand?" and "How secure are the foundations of knowledge in science and mathematics?" Questions can also be as specific as "How did you figure that one out?" or "What does it mean?" The wording may be changed, but children are never too young to analyze the underlying assumptions that influence meanings. And they are never too young to question the interpretation of findings and participate in the act of knowledge creation.

There is always the danger of weakening creative and innovative possibilities. We undermine our chances by getting caught up in what David Whyte calls

> the eddies and swirls of everyday existence.
> I turned my face for a moment and it became my life.

Reasoning, criticism, logical analysis, searching for supporting evidence, and evaluating outcomes might all be considered part of critical thinking. Activities that support this involve clarifying problems, considering alternatives, strategic planning, problem solving, and analyzing the results. Creative thinking may be viewed as fluency, flexibility, originality, and elaboration.

The skills developed in this area would result in the creation of unique expressions, original conceptions, novel approaches, and demonstrations of the ability to see things in imaginative and unusual ways. Problem solving and implementation are part of the fabric of all thinking skills. Enriching the minds of our students involves encouraging them to develop skills that lead to high-quality creative and innovative thinking/applications.

Thinking Across Subjects and in Everyday Life

One way to look at modes of thought across disciplines is through *symbolic*, *imagic*, and *affective* thinking. *Symbolic* includes using words, numbers, and other symbol systems. *Imagic* is visual, spatial, tonal, and kinesthetic. It involves the kind of imagery used by mathematicians and architects, sound relationships explored by musicians, and the movement found in sports and dance. *Affective* thinking works with emotions and feeling to direct inquiry. All three modes of thinking build on reasoning and intuiting to connect the analytic to the intuitive.

As Microsoft founder Bill Gates suggested, "You need to understand things in order to invent things beyond them." The power of inquiry in math, science, and technology lies in its possibility for building on alternative ways of knowing. Along with open-ended problem solving, inquiry also encourages diversity of thought and increases the chances of making creative connections. Creativity might be changing how a particular subject is studied or changing some of the elements of one's personal life.

An innovative mathematician might change the way mathematics is applied to scientific and technological problems. In our personal lives, for example, this could mean changing day-to-day practices to allow for an hour of exercise to improve the general quality of life. An example that is more relevant to children and young adults at school would be clever hypothesis formation.

Effective instruction in mathematics, science, and technology provokes students to create their own questions and think of innovative applications in the world outside of school. As students become interested in such intellectual invention, it is important that the teachers hold off on their judgments and let the evidence itself be the judge.

Mathematicians, scientists, and technology workers use the tools of science and mathematics to collect, examine, and think about data. Conclusions are formulated and outcomes explained. Like scientists, students can reason, analyze, criticize, and advocate—while avoiding dangerous materials and problems that are developmentally inappropriate.

They can also learn to be spontaneous, flexible, and original in their thinking. An understanding of the physical and biological universe is most

solid when it builds on a child's own experiences and discoveries. By modeling thoughtful behavior, teachers can help students become self-confident
enough to resolve inconsistencies and uncover truths in mathematics, science, and technology.

Developing methods that extend creative, critical, and innovative thinking
across the curriculum strategy should be supported by subject matter standards. Making thinking skills part of math and science instruction involves
developing the ability to assess information and make creative and critical
judgments.

Some teachers integrate thinking skills into each subject in the curriculum. Others directly teach children thinking skills and strategies. Using metacognitive (thinking about thinking) strategies is a second approach. Another
conceptual framework synthesizes all three and adds the heavy use of visual
images to soften the boundaries of subject matter and encourage thinking
across disciplines. Of course, many teachers pragmatically borrow from all
the available possibilities to tailor their own lessons for interdisciplinary
inquiry in mathematics, science, and technology.

Multiple Thinking Points to Knowledge

Recognizing thinking skills as directly involved in successful learning
throughout the curriculum does not come as a surprise to most teachers.
There is, however, a tendency to think of the scientific method and mathematics problem solving as clear and clean: you formulate hypotheses, organize experiments, collect and analyze data, and interpret the findings.

As scientists, mathematicians, and engineers who are doing original work
will tell you, the reality is far less clear-cut and tidy. There are many false
starts and detours as they work through alternatives to discover relationships
and invent new perspectives. What makes it satisfying for many scientists is
the sheer power of searching at the frontiers of knowledge. This passion for
inquiry and feeling outward into space for new experiences is just as important for children.

Creative and critical thinkers tend to be reflective as they think problems
through, flexible when they consider original solutions, and curious as they
pose new questions. The research evidence suggests that giving students
multiple perspectives and entry points into subject matter increases thinking
and learning (Costa and Kallick, 2009). The implication here is that ideas
about how students learn a subject need to be pluralized.

Almost any important concept can be approached from multiple directions—emphasizing understanding and making meaningful connections across subjects. This means making learning possibilities and resources (human and technological) available that might appeal to pupils with very different learning styles and cultural backgrounds.

Tomorrow's schools will need to incorporate frameworks for learning that build on the multiple ways of thinking and representing knowledge. By organizing lessons that respect multiple entry points to knowledge, teachers can enhance thoughtfulness and make the school a home for inquiry. If many of today's dreams, possibilities, and admired models are going to be put into widespread practice, then we all must be more courageous in helping move good practice from the margins into the schools, the media, and the home.

A child's thinking ability evolves through a dynamic of personal abilities, social values, academic subjects, and out-of-school experiences. We are all involved, directly or indirectly, in the education of children. Revitalizing the educational process means recognizing the incomplete models of how the world works that children bring to school with them. From birth, children are busy making sense of their environment. They do this by curiously grappling with the confusing, learning ways of understanding, developing schemes for thinking, and finding meaning.

As they enter school, children can sing songs, tell stories, reason in unique ways, and intuit how their surroundings work. By the time they reach first grade, they have already developed a rich body of knowledge about the world around them. The best beginning can be extended in school when the teacher cultivates a broad disposition to critical thinking throughout the year. Working with natural rhythms is important, but it takes learning-centered instruction to continue the process of developing mature thinkers.

Constructivism: Joining Thinking, Content, and Experience

By viewing individual reality as building on real-life experiences, this book borrows heavily from the constructivists. Briefly, constructivism is a learning theory that suggests knowledge is most effectively acquired by evoking personal meaning in the learner. Although there are differences in terminology, there are many similarities with Piagetian theory.

Math, science, and technology lessons may begin with real materials, invite interactive learning, and allow children to explore the various dimensions of thoughtfulness, subject matter, and real-world applications. The goal is to help children construct a new set of expectations and establish a new state of understanding.

When students make sense of something by connecting to a set of personal everyday experiences, constructivists may call it "viable knowledge." Regardless of whether they are familiar with the terms being tossed about, good teachers have always connected academic goals to practical problem solving and students' life experiences. Using such a real-world base embeds thinking skills into the curriculum so that students are intensely involved in reasoning, elaboration, hypothesis formation, and problem solving. Such inquiry-based learning cannot be isolated within rigid disciplinary boundaries.

Developing mature thinkers who are able to acquire and use knowledge means educating minds rather than training memories. Sometimes the acquisition of enhanced thinking skills can be well structured and planned; at other times, it is a chance encounter formed by a crazy collision of elements. The ability to raise powerful interdisciplinary questions about what is being read, viewed, or heard is a dimension of thinking that makes a powerful contribution to the construction of meaning.

When motivated to reason intelligently, children come up with good decision-making options and elaborations. Out of this come insightful creations that suggest possibilities for action. As all of these elements come together, they form the core of effective thinking and learning.

DIMENSIONS OF THINKING

Complex sequences of thinking are required to explore the physical and biological universe. Really proficient learners almost automatically integrate elements of efficient thinking into their repertoire of techniques for making meaning. Students who know the subject and can reason well are less likely to get caught up in scientific misconceptions.

For those who do not find critical and creative thinking quite so automatic, there is good news. Most of these skills can be developed and amplified by effective instruction. There is strong evidence that many students—especially the youngest and lower achievers—need explicit and sustained instruction to become skilled in thinking and monitoring their own thinking processes (Epstein and Rogers, 2001).

In addition to teaching about specific thinking skills, students need guidance in how to apply these skills to science/math inquiry. Mental autonomy, creative expression, and critical thinking develop most fully when connected to the child's home and school environments. Good intellectual habits and arousing a passion for math, science, and technology are the best antidotes for the many flavors of pseudoscience.

Content knowledge, critical thinking skills, and certain clarity of logic have proven to be the best antidotes against innumeracy and pseudoscience. Thinking processes can help us sort out the real from the unreal. They can also help us as we move toward the acquisition of scientific knowledge.

Key indicators of teaching for thoughtfulness include the following:

1. Students are given sufficient time to think before being required to answer questions.
2. Interaction focuses on sustained examination of a few topics rather than superficial coverage of many.
3. The teacher presses students to clarify or justify their opinions rather than accepting and reinforcing them indiscriminately.
4. Interactions are characterized by substantive coherence and continuity.
5. The teacher models the characteristics of a thoughtful person. This means showing interest in students' ideas and their suggestions for solving problems, modeling problem-solving processes rather than just giving answers, and acknowledging the difficulties involved in gaining a clear understanding of problematic topics.
6. Students generate original and unconventional ideas in the course of the interaction. (Perkins, 2010)

Workshops on critical and scientific thinking often focus on four or five dimensions. Many focus on the positive learning attitudes toward thinking that lead to the acquisition and integration of knowledge. This way, content is tied to the teaching of thinking.

The basic idea is to work toward developing the thinking involved in refining and extending knowledge, productive habits of the mind, and the thoughtful use of knowledge. Regardless of the approach, the six steps shown above have proven popular with math and science educators. This is partly because they are compatible with content, collaborative interaction, and what teachers are learning about mathematical reasoning, scientific processes, problem solving, and real-world applications.

THE DIMENSIONS OF GOOD THINKING
AND STAFF DEVELOPMENT

Implementing new approaches to learning about mathematics, science, and technology depends on teachers who are open to new ideas and purposely invite reflective thinking. This means that both prospective and practicing teachers need some practical experiences in problem solving and inquiry. Workshops, conferences, and university-level classes can help. This is especially true if they provide a way for teachers to learn how to apply mathematical and science concepts within a context similar to the one they will use with their students.

When carried out over time, professional development activities have proven useful in helping teachers organize instruction to accommodate new ways of representing and imparting knowledge (Esquith, 2013). Clearly, the result of good *pre-* and *in*-service work expands horizons and organizational possibilities.

Critical and creative thinking are natural human processes that can be amplified by awareness and practice. Creative, critical, and innovative thinking makes use of core thinking skills. Classroom instruction and guided practice in the development of these skills will include the following:

1. *Focusing Skills*—attending to selected chunks of information. Some focusing skills include defining, identifying key concepts, recognizing the problem, and setting goals.
2. *Information-Gathering Skills*—becoming aware of the substance or content needed. Observing, obtaining information, forming questions, and clarifying through inquiry are some skills of information gathering.
3. *Remembering Skills*—involving information storage and retrieval. Encoding and recalling are thinking skills that have been found to improve retention. These skills involve strategies such as rehearsal, mnemonics, visualization, and retrieval.
4. *Organizing Skills*—arranging information so it can be understood or presented more effectively. Some of these organizing skills consist of comparing, classifying (categorizing), ordering, and representing information.
5. *Analyzing Skills*—classifying and examining information of components and relationships. Analysis is at the heart of critical thinking.

Recognizing and articulating attributes and component parts, focusing on details and structure, identifying relationships and patterns, grasping the main idea, and finding errors are elements of analysis.

6. *Generating Skills*—using prior knowledge to add information beyond what is known or given. Connecting new ideas, inferring, identifying similarities and differences, predicting, and elaborating add new meaning to information. Generating skills involve such higher-order thinking as making comparisons, constructing metaphors, producing analogies, providing explanations, and forming mental models.

7. *Integrating Skills*—putting things together, solving, understanding, forming principles, and composing and communicating. These thinking strategies involve summarizing, combining information, deleting unnecessary material, graphically organizing, outlining, and restructuring to incorporate new information.

8. *Evaluating Skills*—assessing the reasonableness and quality of ideas. Skills of evaluation include establishing criteria and proving or verifying data. (Gregerson et al., 2013)

Students have to be able to do more than find information. They also have to be able to evaluate information in a rapidly changing technological environment. Whether it is a website or book, the first step is questioning the source. It is important to build knowledge based on quality information. When using Wikipedia, for example, it is important to know that anyone with access to the Internet can contribute.

Eventually, someone corrects false information, but students need to critically question what they read. Regardless of the source, it is important to *verify* what is found by checking several other sources before seriously considering information.

For teachers to build a solid base of thinking skills into daily math, science, and technology lessons, they must consciously question and reflect on the best approach. Introspective questions about the characteristics of effective instruction help—for example, "How can I get students to focus their thinking, ask questions, retrieve new information, and generate new ideas for analysis?"

To generate ideas, try the following: Think of something and combine it with something else. Adapt whatever you came up with in a way that changes it. Put it to some other use. Eliminate some small part and go on to reverse or rearrange it. What new or innovative ideas emerge?

Multiple Ways of Thinking and Applying

Beyond using manipulatives in math and inquiry in science, teachers are bringing these subjects to life by setting thoughtful application problems in real-life contexts. Knowledge is particularly useful when it can be applied or used to create new knowledge. Students need opportunities to use their knowledge to compose, make decisions, solve problems, and conduct research to discover more. As teachers facilitate activities built on multiple ways of reasoning, doors are opened to the physical and biological universe.

The infusion of creative and innovative thinking into the math and science curriculum goes hand in hand with the basic principles students must learn to be competent in these subjects. Solid reasoning supports the foundation of interdisciplinary inquiry, real-world applications, and the production of new knowledge.

In our efforts to bring science and math to life by making it relevant to students' daily lives, it is important to leave spaces in which students and teachers can reflect on what they are doing and figure out where they will use the skills they are learning. Creativity and innovation have as much to say to government, business, and education as they do to creative fields like the arts and sciences.

People who think creatively have the ability to produce and consider many alternatives—creating or elaborating on original ideas. Creative and innovative thinkers have the ability to see multiple solutions. Developing and expressing emotional awareness is also a part of creative thinking. This is frequently done by perceiving and creating vivid, strong, and lively images from both internal and external vantage points.

Making use of imagination, movement, and sound in playful and useful ways is another element of creative thinking. Overcoming limitations and creating new solutions using humor, predicting consequences, and planning ahead are other elements. While mathematics and science can lead you toward truth, only imagination can lead you to meaning.

Students will learn elements of creative and innovative thinking from interpersonal communication behaviors. These are developed in a variety of ways: listening, speaking, arguing, problem solving, clarifying, and creating (Berry, 2013). Pairs of students can argue an issue with other pairs and then switch sides.

The chaos and dissonance of group work can help foster thinking and imaginative language development. This way, students learn to work creatively with conflicts, viewing them as possibilities for the improvement of literacy. Hopefully, some of this will carry over to conflict resolution and peer resolution of other disputes.

Thinking does not thrive in a threatening and intimidating environment, in which either adult or peer pressure impedes independence. Classrooms organized for creative math and science group work can easily learn to function as a community that respects and supports individual learners.

Good teachers support diverse thinking styles and collaboration, helping all students to think and step outside of subject matter and experience boundaries to construct meaning. This means that the teacher and students open themselves up to suggestions, styles of thinking, connections, and ambiguities previously unexamined. The potential for imaginative action grows out of this process. As Aristotle suggested, there are two steps to doing anything: *Make up your mind* and *Do it!*

Encouraging the Development of Thinking Skills

The test of a first-rate intelligence is the ability to hold two opposed ideas in the mind at the same time, and still function.

—F. Scott Fitzgerald

For the twenty-first century, the ability to do a whole host of complicated tasks at the same time (multitasking) may prove crucial. For those who have difficulty even walking and chewing gum at the same time, there is trouble ahead. The multidimensional search for meaning is made easier when there is a supportive group climate for generating questions and investigating possibilities.

Critical and creative thinking questions may also come into play after solutions are put forward. Ask students to analyze problems they have solved. As they examine how underlying assumptions influence interpretations, children can be pulled more deeply into a topic. And by evaluating their findings on the basis of logic, there arise other possibilities.

The following encourage the development of thinking skills:

• Provide opportunities for students to explore different viewpoints and domains of information that arouse frustration or outrage.
• Conduct debates and discussions on controversial issues that somehow connect to science, mathematics, and technology. Students work in groups to present an argument on a topic and present their view to another group.

Sides can then be switched, the opposite view defended, and different routes to a better social order explored.

- Have students role-play historical events or current news happenings from conflicting viewpoints. Examine some of the more questionable television news images or odd points made about current events on a website whose the power may be palpable but whose connection to reality is tenuous.
- Encourage students to explore Internet websites that present different viewpoints. For homework, you might have them watch a newscast or program on TV (e.g., those that interview individuals with differing perspectives on a problem).
- Have students write letters to a newspaper editor, TV producer, congressman, popular journal, or website expressing their stance on an issue of importance.

These suggestions open up the possibility for developing thinking by practicing argumentative thinking skills in small groups. The basic goal is to stimulate and encourage a wide range of collaboration, divergent thinking, and discussion. By arguing important moral dilemmas in science, medicine, technology, politics, literature, art, music, or sports, students can learn content, reason possibilities, and extend ethical concepts.

To have power over the story that dominates one's life in these technologically intensive times means having the power to retell it, deconstruct it, joke about it, and change it as times change. Without this power, it is much more difficult to think and act on new thoughts and open the doors to deep thinking.

Beyond specific teaching strategies, the climate of the classroom and the behavior of the teacher are very important. Teachers need to model critical thinking behaviors—setting the tone, atmosphere, and environment for learning.

Being able to collaborate with other teachers can make a formative contribution to how the teacher might better see and construct individual classroom reality. Through collaborative problem solving and inquiry, teachers can help each other in the clarification of goals. They can also share the products of their joint imaginations. Thus perceptions are changed, ideas flow, and practice can be meaningfully strengthened, deepened, and extended. Like their students, teachers can become active constructors of knowledge.

Encouraging Innovative Thinking: One Teacher's Checklist

- In what situations did students have to deal with more than one possibility?
- In what ways were students asked to think of new ideas or approaches?
- In what situations were students encouraged to take reasonable risks?
- How were critical and creative thinking skills apparent in the classroom?
- How were multiple intelligences and learning styles considered?
- How often were guessing, hypothesizing, and collaboration encouraged?

The old view of teaching as the transmission of content has been expanded to include new intellectual tools and new ways of helping students thoughtfully construct knowledge on their own and with peers. Teachers who invite thoughtfulness understand that knowledge is to be shared or developed rather than held by the authority. They arrange mathematics instruction so that children construct science/math concepts *and* develop their thinking skills. As a result, everyone involved becomes an active constructor of knowledge and a more capable and thoughtful decision maker in the future.

Recognizing the development of thinking skills is a good first step toward its application and assessment. Some possible guideposts for assessing the development of self-reliant thinking and collaboration include the following:

- A decrease in "How do I do it?" questions (students asking group members before asking the teacher)
- Using trial-and-error discovery learning without frustration
- Questioning peers and teachers (asking powerful why questions)
- Using metaphor, simile, and allegory in speaking, writing, and thinking
- Developing interpersonal discussion skills for shared inquiry
- Increasing ability to work collaboratively in cooperative groups
- Increasing willingness to begin a task
- Initiating inquiry
- Increasing comfort with ambiguity and open-ended assignments
- Synthesizing and combining diverse ideas

It is hard to measure attitudes, thinking, and interpersonal skills on a paper-and-pencil test. Another way is to observe the humor, anecdotes, parental reactions, and teacher-student interactions.

The ability of both students and teachers to pull together as a team influences how well students reflect on their thinking, pose powerful questions, and connect diverse ideas. Failure to cultivate these aspects of thinking may be a major source of difficulty when it comes to learning content.

Powerful Ideas Can Illuminate Learning

A curriculum that ignores students' powerful ideas will miss many opportunities for illuminating the human condition. Teaching content without regard for self-connected thinking prevents subject matter knowledge from being transformed in the student's mind.

When it comes to teaching math, science, and technology, lessons that open doors to the unfamiliar and reasoned decision making are just as important as developing specific knowledge and skills. In addition, a curriculum that takes students' thinking seriously is more likely to be successful in cultivating thoughtfulness *and* subject matter competence.

Respecting unique thought patterns and ideas can also be viewed as a commitment to caring communication and openness. Breaking out of established patterns can be done collectively or individually by those most directly involved. All of us need the occasional push or encouragement to get out of our routines.

It is important for teachers to develop their own reflection, problem-solving, and inquiry skills so they can become students of their own thinking. When a teacher decides to participate with students in learning to think on a daily basis, human possibilities are nourished. Can teachers make a difference? Absolutely.

The idea is to connect willing teachers with high-quality methods and materials so they can build learning environments that are sensitive to the growing abilities of students to think for themselves. Whether it is new technology or anything else, be skeptical unless there are serious studies supporting claims of success.

There are specific skills and approaches that can increase both content mastery and reasoning ability. For example, students' imaginations can be stimulated when they work with content by encouraging them to challenge assumptions, reframe problems, and combine concepts.

By promoting thoughtful learning across the full spectrum of personalities and ways of knowing, teachers can make a tremendous difference and perform a unique service for the future. When the ideal and the actual are linked, the result can produce a dynamic, productive, and resilient form of learning.

What we know is that teaching and thinking are increasingly being put into practice in a growing number of classrooms and schools (Trefil, 2008).

Today's standards-driven programs recognize that powerful problem solving and inquiry can help students make the kind of personal discoveries that change thinking.

Math, science, and technology learning can be amplified when they are coupled with the intellectual tools of creative and innovative thinking. Unleashing such a potential can turn unexamined beliefs into reasoned ones.

Think-Pair-Share Discussion Points for Teachers

When you try to explain something to someone else, you clarify your own thinking and learn more yourself. It helps the learning process when observations and experiences are integrated into a personal framework (memories, associations, feelings, sounds, rules, etc.). The basic idea is to make sure that an individual improves her or his ability to explain, predict, provide analogies, make connections, and consider different perspectives.

By nurturing informed thinking and awareness, teachers can help students learn how to actively apply knowledge, solve problems, and enhance conceptual understanding. Also, as children use these processes to change their own theories and beliefs, they grow in ways that are personally meaningful. In developing conceptual understanding by looking at math and science from new angles, students integrate content and thinking skills into their personal experience.

1. Develop Thinking Skills

Students who are exposed to a variety of viewpoints through various media and authentic materials need to be able to view the varying perspectives critically. Active learning, the nurturing of critical-thinking skills, rather than passive listening, will enable students to develop self-reliance in analyzing both literature and the media.

One means of encouraging active learning is to shift the focus from a teacher-centered approach to one that is student centered. Within this framework, the teacher serves as a facilitator of thinking, rather than an authority figure who transmits knowledge. Instead of the traditional lecture/question approach, students are assigned a specific investigative task that can be accomplished through active teamwork.

2. Shift the Learning Emphasis

In the student-centered class, the emphasis shifts from product to process, from a goal-oriented approach to learning to one in which the learning process is itself the central focus. Less really can be more when it comes to thoughtful connections to science, math, and technology content.

Learning involves not merely the acquisition of information but also the development of critical skills for evaluating and interpreting facts. Sharing various interpretations of a text adds an extra dimension in the learning process as students not only learn how others perceive a certain issue but also appreciate the various reasoning processes and life experiences that support a different interpretation.

3. Teach Thinking Skills

The thinking skills that can be developed include questioning the presentation of information, the order in which facts are presented, the emphasis of certain facts over others, and the implicit slant of any "story," whether it be in literature, science books, or the mathematically based items (charts, graphs, polls, etc.) in the news. Students can also learn to look for discrepancies between the facts and the conclusions drawn from them or inconsistencies among the various versions of a particular news story.

When reading about scientific discoveries, learners can discuss the varying perspectives among the characters and, for older students, the different points of view between the narrator and the characters. It is important to learn how to distinguish between fact and opinion. Is there any totally objective presentation of information?

4. Analyze Stereotypes

As students learn about the perspectives of other cultures, the varying interpretations of breakthroughs in science, mathematics, and technology should be included. Technological developments in times of war—from the atomic bomb in the United States to V2 rockets in Germany—may be viewed as necessity being the mother of invention.

Students may critically view their own culture's interpretation of such events and explore where stereotypes come from. In this framework, each student's cultural background is viewed as a valuable tool for learning, a bridge to another worldview, rather than as a barrier to understanding another individual.

Understanding the essence of the argument means understanding some of the universal truths that speak to everyone *and* recognizing how a diversity of new voices can add vigor to learning. As students learn about the perspectives of other cultures—including social and historical background—they can explore where stereotypes come from.

Supplying students with the common and universal roots of present conditions helps them understand the world and themselves better. Gaining a more integrative understanding of human community leads to an appreciation of overlapping cultural experiences. Also, active learning techniques allow students to collaboratively shape alliances and view each other's cultural background as a valuable tool for learning.

5. *Explore Historical Questions*

A middle-school example is "How might the Renaissance boom in art and architecture be traced to Italian bankers' application of Eastern and Arabic mathematics to finance?"

Why is the history of science full of innovative ideas that several people had at about the same time? Have your students find and explore some examples.

6. *Use Moral Dilemma (Debate) Activities*

Argument (debate) may make some people uncomfortable, but it does result in an understanding of the issues. Bringing important controversial issues out in the open is central to the health and vitality of American education. Encouraging students to argue together can help them reason together (just make sure that each side has an equal chance to be heard). You can get a wide range of interesting responses from questions like the following:

"What does it mean to be human?"
"What might the world be like in twenty-five years?"
"Is the ability to connect with just about anyone at any time worth the invasion of privacy?"

7. *Data Collection and the Erosion of Privacy*

There is usually no requirement to keep records, but when they are kept, they are fair game for lawyers and public viewing. With so much information out there, supply creates demand. It is therefore no wonder that journalists are often advised to destroy their notes every few months. When it comes to viewing a website or buying things in a store, there is money to be made from keeping track of what you are doing. The Electronic Frontier Foundation calls this "the surveillance business model."

What do you think of businesses being able to track just about everything you purchase? What do you think about AT&T promising to route your phone calls and not let anyone listen in . . . and then cooperating with the government's massive surveillance of telephone calls and Internet communications? (By the way, some telecommunication companies refused to go along with the request to collect information; others said they would do it only with a warrant.)

ACTIVITIES FOR STUDENTS

"Writing" a Photo Essay on the World of Work

Original photo essays can be done in the community or at school. They involve predicting, observing, analyzing functional relationships, taking pictures, interviewing, and viewing how a variety of occupations apply strategies to solve problems on the job. This activity will help students connect to the world of future work possibilities and understand their relationship to the adult world.

If the school is used, students should include everyone who comes to the school—from firefighters to university supervisors looking in on student teachers. Students might examine magazines, newspapers, the Internet, and company brochures to see how some stories emphasize pictures.

1. Before observing or asking how a person in a particular occupation works, make a list of what you think the person does. Write a paragraph summarizing your predictions.
2. Check on the accuracy of your predictions, and write a paragraph after observing or having a discussion with the subject. Decide how you may have been wrong early on and add new information after observation and/or discussion.

If you can observe the person at work, take ten pictures of your subject doing different things. Use captions to explain what is going on. Emphasize pictures of problems the person has to understand and plans he or she has to devise, carry out, and evaluate. Keeping in mind the results of the first two sections, prepare a set of five general questions to ask the subject—for example, "What do you do at school, and what training did you do to get the job?" Next, ask five specific questions based on what you noticed when you were observing the subject.

A flaw of any kind can create mystery—and mystery leads to a heightened desire to understand.

To structure the photo essay, proceed as follows: First, provide a brief introduction to get your "reader" interested. Next, use six or seven of your favorite pictures, and list the topic and a caption by each photograph. End the work with a paragraph or two summing up the pictures and leaving readers with what you want them to think about. The end result can be photocopied larger, laminated, provided with graphs, and put up in the classroom or around the school.

Clearing Thoughtful Pathways to Math and Science

As far as math and science are concerned, broad misconceptions, naive theories, oversimplified explanations, and stereotyping often rule the day. Just ask students to draw a picture of a mathematician or scientist, and see what they come up with. Start by having individual students create their own drawing, then share with a partner or small group. The final step is having each group present an example to the whole class for discussion.

Be sure they discuss the differences between drawings and reality. Bringing stereotypes or misconceptions to the surface is not all that difficult, but intelligently dealing with the results requires an in-depth and thoughtful awareness of the subject matter.

Clearing up misunderstandings and exploring subject matter realities are more meaningful when students are connected by a variety of paths to real situations. In fact, few concepts are too difficult when the ideas at the heart of a subject have meaning for students' lives. In a search for meaning, teachers and peers can help individuals understand the personally connected nature of a subject—while leaving room to reshape concepts as new information becomes available.

The personal search for understanding thinking (metacognitive awareness) is shaped by the students' attitudes, the subject matter, knowledge of themselves, and their ability to work with others. Topics can be explored using different methods: descriptive accounts, logical/analytical/quantitative methods, and aesthetic expressions in art, dance, or music.

Lessons can be a pattern similar to the following:

- Forming a topic
- Exploring prior knowledge
- Sharing interesting new questions
- Researching a specific knowledge base
- Comparing, reporting, and thinking reflectively about a project
- Expressing the positive and negative conclusions to an audience

For teachers, it is a question of figuring out how to divide their efforts so they can instruct students with different backgrounds, needs, skill levels, and interests.

Inviting Thoughtfulness and Extending Knowledge

Mathematicians and scientists set out to do some combination of *discovering* and *constructing* the truth. Many disciplines may *interpret*, but math and science attempt to *reveal* the realities of the natural world as they exist in an empirical universe. It was Galileo who famously suggested said that *math is the natural language of the universe.*

We are far from having all the answers needed to design a curriculum that invites students into a full and thoughtful understanding of mathematical problem solving, inquiry, and the scientific method (processes). But we do know enough to begin the intellectual adventure. And we know enough to institute educational practices that promote true understanding.

Reflecting, discussing, and cultivating the disposition for thoughtfulness can inform and enrich our teaching. Whether it is the teacher or a student, asking *why* always helps. The same can be said for developing a sense for asking the right questions—and being able to seek the right answer.

A skilled teacher, open to new ideas, can open a number of doors to adventures in imaginativeness and creative perception. The goal is to integrate, extend, refine, and use knowledge meaningfully. This requires skilled teachers to integrate and fit what is known about promoting creativity and innovation into the instructional process. Educators also need all the help they can get as they work to create vital learning communities that foster critical, creative, civic, and moral thought.

Although improvements in teaching alone will not solve some of our most dire social and educational problems, teachers have an absolutely vital role to play in student success. Also, teachers who have a substantial knowledge of pedagogy and subject matter can use their classroom expertise in a manner that gradually legitimizes new approaches. What challenges might your students be facing in the next fifteen or twenty years?

No one can play it safe and easy when it comes to breaking down the barriers between social problems and educational opportunities. The same can be said for mathematical problem solving and scientific inquiry. Courage and support are needed for individuals to take intelligent risks.

After Thomas Edison made more than ten thousand unsuccessful efforts to develop an electric lamp, he famously said, "I have not failed. I have just found ten thousand ways that won't work." The lesson here is that when you have a setback, keep adapting and *do* something about it. Yes, there are times when it is best to let a problem wither on the vine and go on to more important things. But just as often, when setbacks are relentlessly tackled head on, the results can be amazing.

Both teachers and students should know that, when it comes to innovation, some things work and some things do not. What is important is learning from mistakes. Making mistakes has to be viewed as part of being good at any job. There is, after all, no one else who can fail exactly like you can. So do not waste too much time worrying about it.

Social networks of experienced mentors, teacher educators, and school administrators can provide professional support and have a significant impact on teaching effectiveness (Baker-Doyle, 2011).

Like mathematicians and scientists, teachers can bring about real change in their field only by having the courage, freedom, and support to succeed by sometimes failing. It is much like innovation: some things do work—and some things do not. But if you do not try, enthusiasm can go stale in a hurry.

If given the chance, good teachers, with good approaches, can push the process of more effective thinking and learning forward. Clearly they can make a real difference in helping students learn math, science, technology, and just about everything else.

Good teachers put snags in the river of children passing by, and over the years, they redirect hundreds of lives. Many people find it easy to imagine unseen webs of malevolent conspiracy in the world, and they are not always wrong. But there is also an innocence that conspires to hold humanity together, and it is made of people who can never know the good that they have done.
—Tracy Kidder

VALUING THOUGHTFULNESS

Regardless of whether it is yesterday, today, or tomorrow, a mind equipped to think is one of the most important things for young people to develop.

Subject matter understanding and thinking are not antithetical. Higher-level thinking requires at least some level of content information to be effective. But no textbook, or even the glut of data on the Internet, is a substitute for thinking. So it is important to take the time needed to make sure student thinking reaches a level at which it can transform content knowledge in a way that makes it transferable to the outside world.

Thinking skills are learned through interaction with the school curriculum, environment, peers, and the mass media. Innovative thinkers seek better ways of doing things. They believe in the power of their minds. Some students pick it up naturally, while others learn reasoning skills with difficulty or not at all.

It is clear that at least some thinking skills can be taught directly. For example, generating multiple ideas about a topic, summarizing, figuring out meaning from context, understanding analogy, and detecting reasoning fallacies. Even the length of time a teacher waits ("wait time") after asking a question can make a difference in the quality of a student's thinking. There are times when a three- to five-second pause can add flexibility and creativity to the response (Cole, 2008).

There will *never* be enough time to teach *all* the information we feel is useful. But when there is time for problem solving, inquiry, and reflection, covering less can actually help students learn more deeply. Too much of the math and science curriculum is a little like the Great Salt Lake: roughly twenty miles wide, sixty miles long, and fourteen feet deep. (The size and depth fluctuate substantially due to the shallowness.)

Since it is so difficult to figure out what information will be crucial to students in the future, it makes sense to pay more attention to the *intellectual tools* that will be required in any future. This suggests focusing on how models of critical thought, problem solving, and inquiry can be used differently, at different times, and in different situations.

The idea is to put more emphasis on concepts with high generalizability—like teamwork, reflection, perceptive thinking, self-direction, and motivation needed for lifelong learning. Learning how to learn is important. It is not always what you know, but rather how quickly you can learn it.

Although math, science, and technology are getting more attention than ever, it is important to remind ourselves of the importance of creative and innovative thinking in their own right and in the contributions they can make across the curriculum. For students to learn how to think new thoughts, teachers who recognize children's need to learn in meaning-centered explorations are required.

Serendipity often plays a role in developing creative outcomes, so space is needed for making unexpected discoveries when looking for something else. Feeling and meaning can be turned inside out as children and young adults learn how to construct their own knowledge and absorb new experiences in ways that make sense *to them.*

Promoting creativity and innovation in the classroom requires going beyond giving students the *truth* of others, making it possible for them to discover their own. This somewhat differentiated approach requires teachers to begin instruction where individual students *are* rather than using a uniform model of prescribed lessons.

We know that students learn in a variety of ways and can be encouraged to reach desired goals using very different paths. Children can demonstrate what they have learned about math, science, and technology in a number of ways—through videos, performances, photo collages, stories for the newspaper, blogs on the Internet, or other projects that can be shared with other students and members of the community.

This process gets at the essence of what curriculum is: ways of engaging students in thought on matters that are believed to be important—and sharing what they find. To be educated means knowing the depths that wait for us under the surface of things, regardless of what those things may be.

Thinking and its expression in mathematics, science, and technology can take many forms. Painting, music, and dance (movement) can resonate with meaning and are just one set of neglected imaginative abilities that can be brought to the fore. The idea is to have students work with various media and subject areas so they can go beyond the literal and linear to probe areas that are ambiguous in meaning and rich in illusion. Creative expression is not limited to writing, drawing, or electronic imagery. As Isadora Duncan made clear, "If I could say it, I wouldn't have to dance it."

When the literary converges with the scientific, it is possible to see the universal residing in the particular. Poetry is a powerful way of doing this, while helping you look out over the horizon. "The Summer Day," a poem by Mary Oliver (1992), says as much about imagining the future as it does about the power of observation and the importance of reflecting on the beauty in the natural world. It can be easily accessed on the Internet—just type "Mary Oliver" and "The Summer Day" in a Google search box, and you will get multiple possibilities to click on for the full poem. Among other things, she seems to be asking if there is a better way of spending a day (or more) than in observing, appreciating, and understanding the natural world.

Reflection is one of the keys to higher levels of creative and innovative thinking. It requires a combination of time, silence, and discussion for true appreciation and experience. If you allow yourself to get too hurried, you will lose the ability to pay real attention to the world. The glut of information and increased personal connectivity in today's world can overwhelm children and young adults. This makes taking time for thoughtful reflection—or simply sitting down and reading a book—more difficult than ever.

Innovation involves more than looking at new things in new ways. A source of contemplation for the future can be found in collecting, selecting, and contemplating experiences in the present. Sometimes you can do a better job of figuring out what is going to happen in the future by taking the time to imaginatively look around now, rather than just looking ahead.

> *The real voyage of discovery consists not in seeking new landscapes, but in having new eyes.*
>
> —Marcel Proust

> *Building Diverse Bridges to an Ambiguous Future: Don't tell people how to do things, tell them what to do and let them surprise you with their results.*
>
> —Anonymous

Learning how to think sometimes means cognitive self-observation and taking part in problem solving and inquiry-rich classroom interaction. Being good at creative and innovative thinking means being able to reason and solve new problems. It does not mean repeating memorized words or concepts.

A better approach is engaging in thoughtful instruction that is targeted to the varying learning needs of diverse students. Along the meaning-making way, providing new information and experiences in math- or science-centered subjects can help students adapt and evolve mentally (Kuhn, 2008). Students now have to go beyond knowing to understanding how to actually do something with what they know.

Drawing on past experiences and applying them in innovative ways require that students practice doing so frequently (Wagner, 2012). Expressing, refining, and extending students' reasoning and problem-solving abilities require that teachers and instructional programs take these skills seriously.

When it comes to creative and innovative thinking, teachers can help by modeling the process, stressing firsthand experiences, and arranging class schedules so that there is time for immersion in the more imaginative aspects of mathematics, science, and technology.

The implications of pedagogy extend well beyond the classroom. Educators are at the center of the vision of regaining national momentum; this includes adapting to new realities and inculcating numeracy, scientific literacy, and technological competence at all levels of society.

Continuously reevaluating current knowledge is one of the keys to innovative behavior. Moving students from the conventional to the innovative requires the involvement of informed teachers who can make good use of new approaches and prepare students for unexpected challenges and possibilities. When it comes to individual classrooms, informal belief systems are just as important as methodology.

As teachers become students of their own learning, they discover the inconsistencies between what they *believe* about teaching and how they *practice* the art and science of effective instruction. Such thoughtful reflection about practice can play a major role in helping teachers become autonomous professionals.

Teachers can turn on a spotlight that illuminates how well students are understanding something and go on to make instructional adjustments. Immediate feedback should make it clear how well learning goals are being met and suggest how daily effort can move things along. It also helps to encourage self-regulation to take time to think about how groups and individuals can do better.

At any age, discoveries we make ourselves are more convincing than ones made by others.

Innovative inquiry is not all small-group work. Although open-ended problem solving is the opposite of transmitting information, there will always be a place for teacher presentations and whole-class instruction.

By encouraging learners to work with topics and questions, teachers initiate a good way to arouse innovative curiosity, wonder, and the will to pursue questions that have multiple answers. Questions like "Is the Internet becoming a darker cyberspace that reflects the chaos and bad behavior of today's world, or is it becoming more of a place for learning and healthy adventure?" could be explored.

Other good discussion possibilities about the technological tools of math and science: "If a new Internet were built from scratch, how might security be improved, and how might it be designed to correct some things that the current Internet does poorly, like supporting mobile users?" "What about the privacy and surveillance implications of tracking devices (like smartphones) that are loaded with sensors and always connected to the Internet?" "What are the effects of online browsing, social networking, playing games, and listening to music on a student's productivity in school?" "How well are smartphones doing what laptops, iPads, cameras, and credit cards used to do?"

As science and its math/technology tools play a major role in transforming our world, a more educated public is absolutely essential for dealing with a constantly evolving set of aesthetic, moral, political, and economic issues.

Math and science are disciplines that derive information from specific thought processes: observing, establishing the facts, and proposing rational solutions to problems. After working with peers and hypothesizing from what is known, it may be a good idea to test or confirm the hypothesis. In the past, teachers emphasized the rules of mathematics and science. Now many are making sure that students pay close attention to mathematical problem solving and use scientific methods (processes) of reasoning.

Becoming aware of the outmoded abstractions on which thinking is too often based has a lot to do with mathematical reasoning and scientific inquiry. To paraphrase Alfred North Whitehead, a civilization that cannot break through its current abstractions is doomed to sterility after a very limited burst of progress.

In many ways, there has been a breakdown of the American social and educational compact over the last generation. Basic structures have been unraveled by deregulation, the decline of permanent jobs, and debates taken over by extremes of opinion. Also, the educational system has not kept up with the international competition. There have been previous unwindings and they have been followed by rebuilding. But the context is different now (Packer, 2013).

The performance of U.S. students on international tests would seem to indicate that American schools are doing poorly. Well, some are and some are not. For example, students from middle-class homes in well-funded schools are right up there with the best of the global competition. The overall

U.S. scores are brought down by the fact that the country ranks near the top when it comes to the percentage of children living in poverty.

Good public schools and a more equitable economy are key to a vigorous and informed democracy. And there are plenty of good U.S. educational models out there. But schools are only part of the equation. For every student to achieve academic success, a reduction in poverty and racial isolation is required.

In spite of societal issues, educators can do a lot right now to help students find their way. To reach their full potential, teachers need to stay current, consider different points of view, and look around the corner to see what is coming.

SUMMARY, CONCLUSION, AND LOOKING AHEAD

Teachers are responsible for creating an active learning environment that ensures the maximum growth of every student in their classroom. When it comes to math, science, and technology lessons, it helps to differentiate by carefully attending to student differences, creative interests, and thinking skills.

Good schools make a big difference. But helping young people successfully deal with a rapidly changing, innovation-driven world is a broadly shared social responsibility.

The nation's educational system has been neglected at the very time the need for informed public engagement is growing. Public resources, responsibility, and participation are just as important as making sure teachers are familiar with the characteristics of effective instruction and the subjects they teach.

A broadly informed citizenry is needed to strengthen the national capacity for innovation in an increasingly competitive world. This requires educating *everyone* to think critically, creatively, and deeply.

Largely ignored outliers and people in different fields are often the ones who stimulate you to look at things in different ways (Reynolds, 2012). As far as innovation is concerned, it is helpful to listen closely to people outside of one's usual circle of colleagues and experts. To solve today's problems, especially when new approaches are needed, it is more than rounding up the usual suspects; a range of informed voices must be brought in.

Mathematics, science, and technological applications are bound to be at the center of dramatic twenty-first-century changes. The circumstances of human existence will experience many startling upheavals during the life-span of today's students, so it is no wonder that dealing with complex issues, ambiguity, and unpredictable change are now considered crucial skills for navigating the twenty-first century.

The successful teaching of academic content depends on teachers who have the vision, intellect, and ability to create lessons that include dynamic inquiry and thoughtful problem-solving experiences. The goal is to help students develop the ability to face problems in a new context, self-correct their own thinking, and adapt to change in informed ways.

Today's students have to be prepared to thoughtfully use every tool available to solve the problems of today and tomorrow. They also have to be ready to imaginatively use methods and technologies that have yet to arrive on the scene to solve problems that have yet to be recognized.

Creative alertness, independence, and the ability to fill in missing pieces of a problem puzzle can be taught. Teachers can help by encouraging youngsters to consider alternative viewpoints, figure things out, and draw their own conclusions. Creativity is a renewable resource found in every individual. To flourish, it takes the right environment and interaction with others.

In addition to mastering academic content, it is important to make sure that students' imaginations have enough scope and freedom for their creativity to flourish. Gaining a grade-appropriate mastery of mathematics, science, and technology is essential. But if we ignore the realm of the imagination and its potential impact on the future, we do so at our own peril.

That we have the ability to come up with an endless set of novel responses to the world around us is a constant reminder that we are born to be inventive.
—Tina Seelig (2012)

QUESTIONS FOR TEACHERS AND PROSPECTIVE TEACHERS

1. Successfully dealing with failure is crucial to creativity and innovation. Provide an example of how a personal failure has unleashed creativity.
2. How do you attend to student differences when designing lessons?
3. Explain a good approach for motivating reluctant learners.
4. Did the American social and educational compact break down over the last generation? Explain.

5. Interacting with the world requires creative problem solving every day. What have you done recently that you think is unique?
6. How might you help students develop thinking skills while they are learning math and science? Is there a way digital technology can help?

REFERENCES

Baker-Doyle, K. (2011). *The Networked Teacher: How New Teachers Build Social Networks for Professional Support.* New York, NY: Teachers College Press.

Berry, J. (2013). *You Can Be Creative! A Winning Skills Book.* London, UK: Watkins.

Cole, A. (2008). *Better Answers.* 2nd ed. Portland, ME: Stenhouse.

Copley, A. (2003). *Creativity in Education and Learning: A Guide for Teachers and Educators.* London, UK: Kogan Page.

Costa, A. L., & Kallick, B. (2009). *Habits of Mind Across the Curriculum: Practical and Creative Strategies for Teachers.* Alexandria, VA: Association for Supervision and Curriculum Development.

Epstein, R., & Rogers, J. (2001). *The Big Book of Motivation Games.* Columbus, OH: McGraw Hill.

Esquith, R. (2013). *Real Talk for Real Teachers.* New York, NY: Viking.

Gregerson, M. B., Kaufman, J., & Snyder, H., eds. (2013). *Teaching Creatively and Teaching Creativity.* New York, NY: Springer.

Harlen, W. (2009). *The Teaching of Science in the Primary Schools.* New York, NY: Routledge.

Hooks, B. (2009). *Teaching Critical Thinking.* New York, NY: Routledge.

Kidder, T. (1989). *Among Schoolchildren.* New York, NY: Houghton Mifflin.

Kuhn, D. (2008). *Education for Thinking.* Cambridge, MA: Harvard University Press.

McIntosh, P., & Warren, D. (2013). *Creativity in the Classroom.* Chicago, IL: University of Chicago Press.

Moss, C., & Brookhart, S. (2012). *Learning Targets: Helping Students Aim for Understanding in Today's Lesson.* Alexandria, VA: Association for Supervision and Curriculum Development.

Oliver, M. (1992). "A Summer Day." In *House of Light: New and Selected Poems.* Boston, MA: Beacon Press.

Packer, G. (2013). *The Unwinding: An Inner History of America.* New York, NY: Farrar, Straus, and Giroux.

Perkins, D. (2010). *Making Learning Whole: How Seven Principles of Teaching Can Transform Education.* San Francisco, CA: Jossey-Bass.

Reynolds, L. (2012). *A Call to Creativity.* New York, NY: Teachers College Press.

Robinson, K. (2011). *Out of Our Minds: Learning to Be Creative.* West Sussex, UK: Capstone/Wiley.

Seelig, T. (2012). *inGenius: A Crash Course in Creativity.* New York, NY: HarperOne.

Sternberg, R. (2007). *Wisdom, Intelligence and Creativity Synthesized.* New York, NY: Cambridge University Press.

Trefil, J. (2008). *Why Science?* New York, NY: Teachers College Press.

Wagner, T. (2012). *Creating Innovators: The Making of Young People Who Will Change the World.* New York, NY: Scribner.

Chapter Three

Mathematical Problem Solving

Reasoning and Collaborating in an Age of Data

> *There was a state legislator in Wisconsin who objected to the introduction of daylight saving time. He maintained that if it was instituted, curtains and other fabrics would fade more quickly.*
>
> —John Allen Paulos

Quite a few people have an aversion to mathematics and feel that they would be better off if they could avoid it. As a result, all kinds of misguided ideas stem from policy makers and citizens who do not have a clue when it comes to applying mathematical principles.

No one wants to admit that having problems reading print, but many bright people freely say that they are bad at math. Is literacy is more important than numeracy? The short answer is *no.*

Interacting with the world requires creative mathematical problem solving every day. Whether it is making change at the store or understanding the role of algorithms online, the ability to understand numbers is essential for informed behavior.

At school, there is often a misunderstanding about the difference between arithmetic and mathematics. Traditionally, math instruction focused primarily on the computational skills of arithmetic: addition, subtraction, multiplication, and division—along with whole numbers, fractions, decimals, and percentages. Now digital technology is part of the equation.

Arithmetic matters. But in today's world, a deep understanding of mathematics is much more than facts, figures, and computation. Formalizing, clas-

65

sifying, and dividing things up according to rules are important. But the best math lessons usually go beyond computation and include a formalized version of a natural kind of problem solving.

Everyone should realize that math skills are the foundation for solving both common and complex mathematical problems. One of the many challenges for teachers is teaching mathematical reasoning skills in a way that helps students develop a positive and confident attitude toward mathematics.

Computer-based technology can help—and it deserves attention in math class. Still, how far digital technology can take us in the direction of comprehending a subject is an open question.

Instead of looking at the complex realities, too many people offer the Internet and its tech associates as a simple fix for just about everything. Today's schools face many problems; computers and the Web can help. But inflating the positive possibilities of technology can get in the way of the hard work and public participation required to produce a desirable educational future.

Mathematical algorithms are an example of how math plays a major role in the increasing digitization of our lives. So it is little wonder that an important twenty-first-century skill is the ability to deal with the implications of the engulfing technologies that are being built with mathematical tools.

Developing a more thorough understanding of math, science, and technology is essential, but it takes more to make many of the most important decisions that impact us as humans. For example, the intellectual tools of the arts, the humanities, and the sciences are all needed to move students in the direction of the habit of continuous learning and personal development.

MATH, CREATIVITY, AND THE COMMON CORE STANDARDS

Coming up with new ideas is facilitated by identifying mathematical implications and trying out as many things as possible is a good way to increase the chances of success.

In both the mathematics and the language arts curriculum, the new Common Core State Standards emphasize critical thinking and analytical skills (Marzano and Simms, 2013). Like the earlier National Council of Teachers of Mathematics Standards, there is an emphasis on solving problems in teams. For example, incomplete information about a problem is given to small groups of students and they have to collaborate, fill in the information gaps, and come up with imaginative solutions.

Examples of what teachers might explore:

- The nature of math, mathematical reasoning, and reaching reluctant learners
- Collaborative learning, math inquiry, and building new knowledge
- The content standards and the implications for all of their students
- Problem-solving strategies and activities for implementing the standards
- The technological implications of measurement and big data in a digital age

Typically, learners bring widely varying backgrounds to their math lessons, and teachers work hard to accommodate this diversity. On one level, we believe that all students have the potential to learn mathematics. On another level, we all have to admit that at least some of our students arrive so unprepared that they encounter academic difficulties.

Everyone from math educators to textbook writers has been working hard to develop creative and innovative ways to meet the mathematical needs of reluctant learners. Students with attention deficits, memory problems, motor disabilities, and visual or auditory difficulties are just some of challenges for teachers.

Whatever a student's strength or weakness, many will require special accommodations in the math classroom to reach their full potential. Accommodations often go beyond physical and environmental difficulties. In today's diverse classrooms, we often find English-language learners and others who simply need further basic math instruction.

With some struggling students, it is not a question of language proficiency or disability, but rather a question of motivation and attitude. Whatever the source of difficulty, providing reluctant math learners with a strong mathematics program will be easier if the teacher is able to adjust instruction, build teamwork skills, and tap into the natural strength of each student (Bender, 2013).

It is best to make sure that even the most reluctant learner understands what it means to *know* and *do* mathematics *in* and *out* of school. Inventing the future may be asking too much. But still, all students can learn to use mathematical reasoning and applications to question the world as it is and make a contribution to how it should be.

The Nature of Mathematics

Mathematics may be defined as follows:

1. *Mathematics is a method of thinking and asking questions.* How students make math-related plans, organize their thoughts, analyze data, and solve problems is *doing* mathematics. People comfortable with math are often comfortable with thinking. *The question* is the cornerstone of all investigation. It guides the learner to a variety of sources revealing previously undetected patterns. These undiscovered openings can become sources of new questions that can deepen and enhance learning and inquiry.

2. *Mathematics is a knowledge of patterns and relationships.* Students need to recognize the repetition of math concepts and make connections with ideas they know. These relationships help unify the math curriculum as each new concept is interwoven with former ideas. Students quickly see how a new concept is similar or different from others already learned. For example, students soon learn how the basic facts of addition and subtraction are interrelated ($4 + 2 = 6$ and $6 - 2 = 4$). They use their observation skills to describe, classify compare, measure, and solve problems.

3. *Mathematics is a tool.* It is what mathematicians use in their work. It is also used by all of us every day. Students come to understand why they are learning the basic math principles and ideas that the school curriculum involves. Like mathematicians and scientists, they will also use mathematics tools to solve problems. They will learn that many careers and occupations are involved with the tools of mathematics.

4. *Mathematics is fun (a puzzle).* Anyone that has ever worked on a puzzle or stimulating problem knows what we are talking about when we say mathematics is fun. The stimulating quest for an answer prods one on toward finding a solution (House, 2013).

5. *Mathematics is an art*, defined by harmony and internal order. Mathematics needs to be appreciated as an art form in which everything is related and interconnected. Art is often thought to be subjective, and by contrast, objective mathematics is often associated with memorized facts and skills. Yet the two are closely related to each other.

   Because teachers tend to focus on the skills, they may forget that students need to be guided to recognize and appreciate the fundamental organization and consistency as they construct their own understanding of mathematics. Students need to be taught how to appreciate the mathematical beauty all around them.

6. *Mathematics is a language*, a means of communicating. It requires being able to use special terms and symbols to represent information. This unique language enhances our ability to communicate across the disciplines of science, technology, statistics, and other subjects. For example, a struggling learner encountering $3 + 2 = 5$ needs to have the language translated into terms he or she can understand. Language is a window into students' thinking and understanding. Our job as teachers is to make sure students have carefully defined terms and meaningful symbols.

    Statisticians may use mathematical symbols that seem foreign to some of us, but after taking a statistics class, we, too, can decipher the mathematical language. It is no different for children. Symbolism, along with visual aids such as charts and graphs, is an effective way of expressing math ideas to others. Students learn not only to interpret the language of mathematics but also to *use* that knowledge.

7. *Mathematics is interdisciplinary*. Math works with the big ideas that connect subjects. Mathematics relates to many subjects. Science and technology are the obvious choices. Literature, music, art, social studies, physical education, and just about everything else make use of mathematics in some way.

Reluctant learners claim they are just not interested in mathematics, working in groups, or even discussing the seven ways that math, when used every day, can change their views. The following activities may help students like these reluctant learners discover what math is all about and change their minds about math.

Activities that help reluctant groups define mathematics are as follows:

1. *Mathematics as a Method of Thinking*: List all the situations outside of school in which your group used math during the past week.

2. *Math as Knowledge of Patterns and Relationships*: Have your first-grade class show how one math combination (like $4 + 2 = 6$) is related to another basic fact (like $6 - 4 = 2$). Or students in later grades can think about the result that changing the perimeter of figure has on its area.

3. *Math as a Tool*: Solve this problem using the tools of mathematics: A man bought an old car for $50 and sold it for $60. Then he bought the car back for $70 and sold it again for $80. How much money did he make or lose? Do the problem with your group and explain your reasoning.

4. *Math as Having Fun, Solving a Puzzle*: With a partner, play a game of cribbage (a card game in which the object is to form combinations for points). Dominoes is another challenging game to play in groups.

5. *Math as an Art*: With a small group of students, design a picture. Have students find shapes and label them. Students can create a scary or futuristic art picture using geometric shapes.

6. *Math as a Language*: Divide the class into small groups of four or five. Have the group brainstorm about what they would like to find out from other class members (favorite hobbies, TV programs, kinds of pets, and so forth). Once a topic is agreed on, have them organize and take a survey of all class members. When the data are gathered and compiled, have groups make a clear, descriptive graph that can be posted in the classroom.

7. *Math as Interdisciplinary*: With a group, design a song using rhythmic format that can be sung, chanted, or rapped. The lyrics can be written and musical notation added.

COLLABORATIVE MATH INQUIRY

Collaborative inquiry is a way of teaching that builds on group interaction and students' natural curiosity. Inquiry refers to the activities of students in which they develop knowledge and understanding of mathematical ideas. This active process involves students in asking questions, gathering data, observing, analyzing, proposing answers, explaining, predicting, and communicating the results.

Collaborative problem solving is supported when students have opportunities to describe their own ideas and hear others explain their thoughts, raise questions, and explore various team approaches. Within a small-group setting, students have more opportunities to interact with math content than they do during whole-class discussions.

In collaborative problem solving, the role of the teacher is to help students become aware of how to ask questions and how to find evidence. As teachers move away from a "telling" model to "structured group experiences," they encourage students to interact with each other and value social relationships as they become informed investigators.

The challenge for the teacher is to set up group work that engages students in meaningful math activities. Today, even struggling students are being challenged to think and work together to solve problems. The next step is helping them feel secure as they go about applying their understandings.

We want all students to be involved in high-quality engaging mathematics instruction. High expectations should be set for all, with accommodations for those who need them. Students will confidently engage in mathematics tasks, explore evidence, and provide reasoning and proof to support their work. As active resourceful problem solvers, students will be flexible as they work in groups with access to technology. Students come to value mathematics when they work productively and reflectively as they communicate their ideas orally and in writing.

Being successful in mathematics is not a highly ambitious dream; rather, it is part of the vision set forth in the National Council of Teachers of Mathematics Standards document.

NCTM Standards for School Mathematics

The standards are descriptors of the mathematical content and processes that students should learn. They call for a broader scope of mathematics studies, pointing out what should be valued in mathematics instruction. The ten standards describe a comprehensive foundation of what students should know and be able to do. They state the understandings, knowledge, and skills required of elementary and middle-school students.

All students should be provided with the opportunity to learn significant mathematics. The Principles and Standards for School Mathematics strengthens teachers' abilities to do that by including information about the way students develop mathematical knowledge. The standards include content (addressing what students should learn) and process (addressing aspects of doing mathematics).

The content standards, number and operations, algebra, geometry, measurement, data analysis, and probability describe the foundations of what students should know. The process standards of problem solving, reasoning and proof, communicating, making connections, and representing data express ways of using and applying content knowledge.

The goals articulated by the standards can be responsive to accelerated changes in our society, our schools, and our classrooms. Individual teachers can make alterations for students within their classrooms, but the school itself must have a coherent program of mathematics study for students. No curriculum should be carved in stone at any level; rather, it must be responsive to the lessons of the past, the concerns of the present, and the human and technological possibilities of the future.

Implementing the Math Standards

Here we connect the standards to classroom practice by presenting few sample activities for each standard. The intent is not to prescribe an activity for a unique grade level, but rather to present activities that can be adapted for many grades.

Number and Number Operations Standard

Concepts and skills related to numbers are a basic emphasis for struggling students. Teachers should help reluctant learners strengthen their sense of numbers, moving from initial basic counting techniques to a more sophisticated understanding of numbers, if they are to make sense of the ways numbers are used in their everyday world. Our number system has been developing for hundreds of years. The modern system we use today grew from many contributions made by numerous countries and cultures.

There are four important features of the number system:

1. *Place value.* The position of a numeral represents its value; for example, the numeral 2 in the numbers 21, 132, and 213 represents different ways of thinking about the value of the number 2. In the first case, 2 represents 2 tens or 20, the second 2 represents 2 ones or 2, and in the third case 2 represents 2 hundreds or 200.
2. *Base of ten.* Base in the number system means a collection. In our number system, ten is the value that determines a new collection. Our number system has ten numerals: 0, 1, 2, 3, 4, 5, 6, 7, 8, 9. This collection is called a *base-ten system.*
3. *Use of zero.* Unlike other number systems, our system has a symbol for zero. Encourage students think about the Roman numeral system. The reason it is so cumbersome to use today is that it has no zero.
4. *Additive property.* Our number system has a specific way of naming numbers. For example, the number 321 indicates the number 300 + 20 + 1.

Place value is one of the most important concepts in the elementary and middle school. Solving problems that involve computation includes understanding and expressing multi-digit numbers. Yet knowing when to exchange groups of ones for tens or what to do with a zero in the hundreds place when subtracting, for example, baffles many students who then struggle with the step-by-step subtraction problem.

Students are helped by solving real-world problems with hands-on materials such as counters, base-ten blocks, and place value charts. Students create meaning for themselves by using manipulatives.

The following place value activities are designed to get reluctant learners actively involved.

Grouping by Tens or Trading

Students may be more motivated when teachers provide more experiences in counting many objects; trading for groups of tens, hundreds, and thousands; and talking together about their findings. Math learners need many models. Bean sticks and base-ten blocks are two models widely used by teachers. But students also need piles of materials (rice, beans, straws, counters, and unifix cubes) to practice counting, grouping, and trading.

Ask students to group by tens as they work. This makes the task of counting easier for students; counting by tens also helps students check errors in their counting. But most importantly, sorting by tens shows students how large amounts of objects can be organized. Some common errors related to place value include not regrouping when necessary or regrouping in the wrong place.

Trading Rules

The base-ten system works by trading ten ones for one ten, or the reverse, trading one ten for ten ones, ten tens for one hundred, ten hundreds for one thousand, and so on. Base-ten blocks are a great ready-made model in teaching this principle. Encourage students to make their own model.

Building models with popsicle sticks and lima beans works equally well. Or if teachers wish to have students use construction paper and scissors, students can make their base-ten models by cutting out small squares of paper and pasting them on a ten strip to form a ten. Then, after completing ten tens, paste the ten strips together to make a hundred, and then paste the hundreds together to form a thousand. It is time-consuming work but well worth the effort.

Proportional models such as base-ten blocks, bean sticks, and ten strips provide physical representation. In all the examples just mentioned, the material for ten is ten times the size of the unit; the hundred is ten times the size of the ten; the thousand is ten times the size of the hundred; and so on. Metric measurement provides another proportional model. Meter stick, decimeter rods, and centimeter cubes can be used to model any three-digit number.

Nonproportional models such as money do not exhibit a size relationship, but rather present a practical real-life model. Because both types of models are important and should be used, we recommend starting students with proportional models, as they are more concrete and help learners to understand the relationships more clearly.

Teaching Place Value

It is important that students think of numbers in many ways. A good place to start is to pass out a base-ten mat with the words "ones," "tens," and "hundreds." Also pass out base-ten blocks to each of the students (units, longs, flats). The units represent ones, longs represent tens, and flats represent hundreds. Now have the students build the number they hear. If, for example, the teacher says the number 42, the students take four long rods (tens) and place them on the tens column of their mat, and two units, placing them in the ones column. Encourage students to test their skill in a small group by thinking of a number, verbalizing it, and then checking other students' mats.

Fractions

Fraction concepts are among the most complicated and important mathematical ideas that students will encounter. Perhaps because of their complexity, fractions are also among the least understood by students. Some of the difficulties may arise from the different ways of representing fractions: spoken symbols, written symbols, manipulative materials, pictures, and real-world situations (Empson and Levi, 2011).

It may be difficult for struggling students to make sense of these five ways of representing fractions and connecting them in meaningful ways. Learners need many chances to work with concrete materials, observe and talk about fractional parts, and relate their experiences to science and mathematical notation. One helpful activity is to have students make a fraction kit.

Make a Fraction Kit

This introductory activity introduces fractions to students. Fractions are presented as parts of a whole.

Materials: Each student needs seven different 3" × 18" strips of colored construction paper, a pair of scissors, and an envelope to put their set of fraction pieces labeled as follows: 1, 1/2, 1/3, 1/4, 1/8, 1/12, 1/16.

Direct students to cut and label the strips:

1. Have students select a colored strip. Emphasize that this strip represents one whole and have students label the strip 1/1 or 1.
2. Ask students to choose another color, fold it in half, cut it, and then label each piece 1/2. Talk about what 1/2 means (1/2 means 1 piece out of 2 total pieces).
3. Have students select another color, and have them fold and cut it into four pieces, labeling each piece 1/4. Again, discuss what 1/4 means (1 piece out of 4 total pieces, compare the 4 pieces with the whole).
4. Have students fold, cut, and label a fourth colored strip into eighths, a fifth strip into twelfths, and a sixth strip into sixteenths.

Now each student has a fraction kit. Encourage students to compare the sizes of the pieces and talk together about what they discover. For example, students can easily observe that the fractional piece 1/16 is smaller than the piece marked 1/4. This is a good time to introduce equivalent fractions: "How many 1/16 pieces would it take to equal 1/4? What other fractional pieces would equal 1/4?" Explaining equivalence with a fraction kit makes fractions more meaningful (Burns, 2001).

Algebra Standard: Patterns and Functions

Patterns are everywhere in everyday life. People organize their home and work activities around patterns. The inclusion of patterns and functions in elementary and middle school opens many possibilities for math instruction. Teachers can connect many ideas in mathematics to students' background knowledge by encouraging them to describe patterns and functions in their own language to help them represent those ideas with mathematical symbols.

Representing functions algebraically calls for the use of variables. Young students first learn about using variables as placeholders for unknown numbers—for example, (__ + 3 = 10) or (5 + n =12). In these situations, variables represent answers—specific nonvarying numbers can be determined by solving the equation.

Later, students learn that variables can be used not only for specific unknown quantities but also for a wide range of values. Equations that use variables in this way can generalize mathematics properties. For example, if a student has described a pattern such as "each object is 3 times more than the last one," they can symbolically represent their idea as *n* (the object) and describe the *nth* object as $n \times 3$.

Patterns and functions naturally lead to an understanding of functions in algebra. In the activities that follow, we will explore only a few types of patterns and functions and ways to describe them. The more opportunities struggling students have to describe patterns and functions with pictures, words, tables, and variables, the more power with mathematics they will have.

Multiplication Activity: Using Algebra to Build Rectangles

Discuss rectangles and demonstrate how to name them—for example, 2×3 (2 rows of 3 units) and 4×5 (4 rows of 5 units). Provide students with a sheet of graph paper.

Directions

Instruct students to plan a design, creature, or scene that they could make using only rectangles. Have them cut the graph paper into rectangles. Use the whole page. Paste the rectangles onto construction paper to make their design. Write a number sentence that tells how many 1 cm $\times$ 1 cm rectangles are included in their design. Since all students started with the same size graph paper, they should all get the same answer, although their equations will be different. If the class uses a 10 cm $\times$ 10 cm graph-paper grid, students can write statements that show what percentage of the whole picture is represented by each part. Have students write stories about their pictures. The stories should include mathematical statements using algebraic notation (Cathcart et al., 2010).

Multiplication Factor Puzzles Activity

Place a large sheet of butcher paper on the chalkboard. Divide the paper, labeling each part with a multiplication product (18, 20, 21, 36, 40, and so on). Divide the class into teams. Ask each team to find and cut out of graph paper all the rectangles that can be made with a given number (20, for example). Have each team label and paste their rectangles on the butcher paper under that number.

As a whole class, review the findings and determine if all the possible rectangles have been found for each number without duplicates (flips, rotations). List the factors for each number.

Geometry Standard

In the elementary grades, geometry should provide opportunities for students to develop the concepts of shape, size, symmetry, and congruence and similarity in two- and three-dimensional space. Reluctant learners should begin with familiar objects and use a wide variety of concrete materials to develop appropriate vocabulary and build understanding.

Construct a Chinese Tangram Puzzle

Materials: Six-inch squares of construction paper, scissors.

The tangram is a Chinese puzzle made from seven geometric shapes. The seven shapes can be put together in hundreds of ways. Tangrams are fun for students to work with in developing spatial concepts. The tangram puzzle is cut from a square. Having students each cut their own is a good lesson in following directions.

Directions for Making a Tangram Kit

1. Fold the square in half. Have students cut it apart to make two triangles.
2. Have students take one triangle and fold it in half and cut.
3. Take the other triangle, and make two folds—first fold in half, and then fold the top corner down. Cut along the folds (students should have one trapezoid and one triangle).
4. Cut the trapezoid in half.
5. Fold one trapezoid to make a square and a triangle. Cut.
6. Fold the last trapezoid to make a parallelogram and a triangle. Cut.
7. Place cut shapes in an envelope.

Tangram Shape Exploration

1. Use the three smallest triangles to make a square. Use the same pieces to make a triangle, a rectangle, a trapezoid, and a parallelogram.

2. Use the five smaller pieces (all but the two large triangles) to make the same shapes.
3. Repeat with all seven pieces.

Evaluation

When students have made a tangram kit of their own, have them put the square together. Encourage them to share their puzzle with family and friends.

Extensions

1. Students can explore using the pieces to make a shape of their own. Have them draw an outline around the shape on drawing paper, name it, sign it, and put it in a class tangram box so that others can solve their puzzles.
2. Area and Perimeter: Encourage students to compare the areas of the square, the parallelogram, and the large triangle. Then have them compare their perimeters and record their findings.

Measurement Standard

Concepts and skills in the measurement standard deal with making comparisons between what is being measured and a standard unit of measurement. Students acquire measuring skills through firsthand experiences. It is important to remind students that measurement is never exact; even the most careful measurements are approximations. Students need to learn to make estimates when measuring.

Measurement tools and skills have many uses in everyday life. Being able to measure connects mathematics to the real-world environment. Being able to use the tools of measurement—rulers, measuring cups, scales, thermometers, meter sticks, and so on—and to estimate with these tools are essential skills for students to develop.

Instruction in measurement should progress through these attributes of measurement: length, weight/mass, volume/capacity, time, temperature, and area. Within each of these areas, students need to begin making comparisons with standard and nonstandard units. In the upper grades, more emphasis can be placed on using measurement tools.

Sample Measurement Activity: Body Ratios

Students need direct concrete experiences when interacting with mathematical ideas. The following activities are designed to clarify many commonly held incorrect ideas:

- *Finding the Ratio of Your Height to Your Head*: How many times do you think a piece of string equal to your height would wrap around your head? Many struggling students have a mental picture of their body, and they make a guess relying on that perception. Have students make an estimate, and then have them verify it for themselves. Few make an accurate guess based on their perceptions.
- *Comparing Height with Circumference*: Have students imagine a soft-drink can, and then instruct them to think about taking a string and wrapping it around the can in order to measure its circumference. Ask students to make guesses as to whether the circumference will be longer, shorter, or roughly the same as the height of the can. Encourage students to estimate how high the circumference measure will actually reach. Then have the students try it for themselves.

  As in the previous activity, many students guess incorrectly. The common misperception is that the string will be about the same length as the height of the can. There is a feeling of surprise or mental confusion when they discover that the circumference is about three times the height of the can. Struggling students feel more confident when they see fellow classmates searching for a correct answer. Repeat the experiment with other cylindrical containers. Have students record their predictions and come up with a conclusion (Burns, 2001).

Group Activity: Estimate, Measure, and Compare Your Shoes

Materials: Unifix cubes, shoes

Procedures

Have the students estimate how many unifix cubes would fit in their shoe. Ask them to write down their estimate. Choose a volunteer from a group to take off his or her shoe. Ask the student estimate how many unifix cubes would fit in the shoe. When finished with the estimate, actually measure the shoe using unifix cubes, and then have the student volunteer record the measurement.

Students might be asked to pass the shoe to the next group and have them estimate and record the actual measurement. Students should continue passing the shoes around the class until all students have recorded estimates and each group has taken actual measurements of the shoes.

Evaluation

Instruct students to compare the shoes. Have students explain what attribute of measurement they used. Encourage students to think of another way to measure the shoes. Explain how it might be more accurate. Get students into pairs or groups of three or four; everyone should be and actively engaged in estimating and measuring each other's shoes.

Metric Perimeter Using Cuisinaire Rods

Materials: Cuisinaire rods, centimeter paper

Procedure

Have students use one red rod (2 cm), two light green rods (3 cm), and one purple rod (4 cm). Have them arrange the rods into a shape on centimeter squared paper in such a way that when students trace around it, they draw only on the grid-paper lines. Students should cut out the shape and have it remain in one piece. Make several different shapes this way. Trace each and record its perimeter. Try to get the longest and the shortest perimeter.

Data Analysis and Probability Standard

It is difficult to listen to the news on television or pick up a newspaper without noticing the extensive use of charts, graphs, probability, and statistics. What follows are a few suggestions for teaching struggling students some elementary concepts for probability and graphing.

The study of data analysis, statistics, and probability invites students to collect, organize, and describe information. Students communicate data through tables, graphs, and other representations. Probability and statistics are mathematical tools for analyzing and drawing conclusions about data.

Classifying and Predicting

Give students a list of statements and ask them to sort them into three piles labeled "certain," "uncertain," and "impossible." Use statements such as the following:

- Tomorrow it will rain.
- I will get 100 percent on my next spelling test.
- Tomorrow we will all visit Mars.
- If I flip a coin, it will land either heads or tails.

As the students classify the statements, discuss with them the reasons for the classifications. When they have finished, ask them to further classify the uncertain statements as either likely or unlikely. In doing this, students are predicting the outcome.

Encourage students to give examples of activities and experiments to clarify their thinking. As a follow-up activity, have students come up with their own list of statements to classify into categories and offer their predictions. Reluctant learners can be encouraged to become active math participants.

Predicting Coins and Colors

Ask students to predict whether a coin will land on heads or tails. Flip the coin and show the result. Ask students to predict the outcome of several flips of the coin. Discuss whether one flip seems to have an influence on the next flip. Events are called independent if one event has no effect on another. Give each student a penny and ask them to make a tally of the heads and tails out of ten flips. Talk about such terms as "equally likely," "random," and "unbiased." Clearly explain the terms. If a student seems confused, have him or her work with a partner.

Show the students a spinner with three colors (red, yellow, blue). Spin the spinner a few times to show that it is a fair spinner. Ask students to predict the number of times they could expect to get yellow if they spin the spinner thirty times. Can they find a formula for predicting the number of times a color will come up? If the probability of landing on each color is equally likely, they can write the probability of landing on any one color as the number of favorable outcomes or the total number of outcomes.

In the example of the spinner, the total number of outcomes is three because there are three colored sections altogether. Therefore, the probability of getting yellow is one out of three, or 1/3. Ask the students to predict the number of times they could expect to get yellow if they were to spin the spinner thirty times.

Try the experiment using different colors and different numbers of spins. Can the students find a formula for predicting the number of times a color will come up?

Exploring Sports Statistics

The following are the salaries of five professional basketball players: $80,000, $80,000, $100,000, $120,000, and $620,000. The players are complaining about their salaries. They say that the mode of the salaries is $80,000 and that they deserve more money for all the games they play. The owners claim the mean salary is $200,000 and that this is plenty for any team. Which side is correct? Is anyone lying? How can students explain the difference in the reports?

Ask students to look in newspapers and magazines for reported averages. Are there any discrepancies in the reports? Bring in reports for discussion in class. Even slow readers respond enthusiastically to this sports challenge. Encourage students to read any reported statistics carefully.

Data Investigation Exercises

In the future, we will all be called upon to approach and solve problems not even envisioned today. A good preparation in mathematics provides the language, the tools, and the computational techniques needed to get the job done. Understanding the conceptual bases of mathematics, having the ability to communicate mathematical ideas to others, and demonstrating mathematical competence will be more important than ever.

A mathematics investigation is more demanding than a problem or an exercise. Sometimes they are used to introduce and learn mathematical concepts. More often, investigations are project-like culminating activities that help students integrate what they are learning into a comprehensible whole. Like the problem, the investigation lets struggling students use several different approaches. It requires students to generate and structure the problem— creating a context that invites sustained work.

Authentic Problems

Authentic problems are those that you actually face, like trying to decide what to order at a restaurant, how to spend your allowance, where to go on your vacation, or how to get through the rest of the semester. These may be some of your real-life problems, but authentic national problems can be found in the newspaper or seen on the news every day.

Making Mistakes

Students need to learn that as long as you try your best, it is okay to fail. Just fail fast, ask yourself how it happened, and see if it is possible to come up with some useful adaptations.

Problem-Solving Standard

Problem solving has been central to elementary mathematics for nearly two decades. Problem solving refers to engaging in a task in which the solution is not known. George Polya, a well-known mathematician, devised a four-step scheme for solving problems: understand the problem, create a strategy or plan, follow through with the approach selected, and check back. Does this scheme make sense?

Problems are teaching tools that can be used for different purposes. The solutions are never routine, and there is usually no right answer because of the multitude of possibilities. Strategies include guessing and checking, making a chart or table, drawing a picture, acting out the problem, working backward, creating a simpler problem, looking for patterns, using an equation, using logic, asking someone for help, making an organized list, using a computer simulation, coming up with your own idea, and taking a risk.

Teachers should model the problem-solving strategies needed for thinking about mathematics content or responding to particular math problems. Modeling might include the thinking that goes into selecting what strategy to use, deciding what options are possible, and checking on their progress as they go along. Reluctant learners can catch on quickly if guided through this process.

What follows are a few problem-solving activities.

Present Interesting Problems

Present a problem to the class. Have students draw pictures of what the problem is about, act out the problem, or read the problem leaving out the numbers. Once students begin to visualize what the problem is about, they have much less difficulty solving it. Students should work in small groups when arriving at strategies and when solving the problems. Students should write how they solved it and discuss and check their answers with other groups.

The following is a sample problem to present to the class:

> *Solve This Problem:*
> One day Farmer Bill was counting his pigs and chickens. He noticed they had 60 legs and there were 22 animals in all. How many of each kind of animal did he have?
> (This is a fun problem for struggling students if they can draw a picture of the animals and think about what the problem is asking.)
> Record your strategy below.

> *Sample Possible Problem:*
> Your two friends slept over last night. You, Tom, and David each ate something different for breakfast. One had fried eggs and toast, one had cereal, and one had a banana split. (The last was allowed because the parents were away on vacation and there was a babysitter who spoiled the boys.) David did not have fried eggs and toast or a banana split. You did not have fried eggs and toast. Whose parents were on vacation?

Suggestions for Enhancing Math Learning

Marilyn Burns and others have suggested a number of ways to improve problem solving in math:

1. *Understanding creates success.* "Do only what makes sense to you."
2. *Encourage students to explain their thinking.* "Ask: Why do you think that? Convince us. Prove it."
3. *Remember students need to communicate together.* "Interaction helps children clarify their ideas, get feedback for their thinking, and hear other points of view."
4. *Have writing be a part of mathematics learning.* "When students write in math class, they have to revisit their thinking and reflect on their ideas."
5. *Real-world activities spark students' interest.* "When connected to situations, mathematics comes alive."
6. *Manipulatives enhance students' learning.* "Manipulative materials help make abstract mathematical ideas concrete."
7. *Math curriculum should support the students.* "Students' understanding is key and does not always happen according to a set schedule."

8. *Good activities involve all students.* "Keep an eye out for activities that are accessible to students with different interest and experience."

9. *Math learning invites confusion.* "The classroom culture should reinforce the belief that errors are opportunities for learning . . ."

10. *Different ways of thinking should be celebrated.* (Burns, 2004)

Communication Standard

Outside the classroom, real-world problems are rarely solved by people working alone. People work in groups and pool their knowledge. Cooperative group learning is a way to help students develop communication skills. Through listening and talking, students learn to express ideas and compare them to those of others. Students listen to explanations and solutions of their peers and obtain information from books and electronic sources. Throughout the elementary and middle-school years, students develop mathematical language using precise terms to describe math concepts and procedures.

Connections Standard

The connections standard emphasizes the many relationships between mathematics topics and everyday life. There are important connections between hands-on and intuitive mathematics. Like everyone else, struggling students need to learn through their own experiences with math. For mathematics to be meaningful, strong connections to experiences outside of school need to be made.

Making Connections (Addition and Subtraction)

When students are learning about the operations of addition and subtraction, it is helpful for them to make connections between these processes and the world around them. Story problems help them see the actions of joining and separating. Using manipulative and sample word problems gives them experience in joining sets and figuring the differences between them. By pretending and using concrete materials, learning becomes more meaningful. Tell stories in which the learners pretend to be animals or things.

BUILDING CONNECTIONS ACROSS DISCIPLINES

During their time in elementary and middle school, students should be developing the processes of scientific inquiry and mathematical problem solving, which include inferring, communicating, measuring, classifying, and predicting. Investigations that connect the two disciplines are problems like these:

1. How many ways can you sort your bag of buttons?
2. Make a Venn diagram using your buttons. Students may need help understanding what a Venn diagram is. Again, modeling and getting struggling students involved working with a group dispels confusion.
3. Classify the buttons. (Notes: light to dark color, small to large, number of ridges, number of patterns, number of holes.)

Representation Standard

Representing ideas and connecting them to mathematics are the bases for understanding. Representations make mathematics more concrete. A typical elementary classroom has several sets of manipulative materials to improve computational skills and make learning more enjoyable.

Base-ten blocks will be used in these activities to represent the sequence of moving from concrete manipulations to the abstract algorithms. Students need many chances to become familiar with the blocks and discover the vocabulary (1s = units, 10s = longs, 100s = flats) and the relationships among the pieces. The following activities will explore trading relationships in addition, subtraction, multiplication, and division.

The Banker's Game (Simple Addition)

In this activity, small groups of students will be involved in representing tens. The game works best dividing the class into small groups (four or five players and one banker). Each player begins with a playing board divided into units, longs, and flats. Before beginning, the teacher should explain the use of the board. Any blocks the student receives should be placed on the board in the column that has the same shape at the top.

A student begins the game by rolling a die and asking the banker for the number rolled in *units*. They are then placed in the units column on the student's board. Each student is in charge of checking his or her board to decide if a trade is possible. The trading rule states that no player may have more than nine objects in any column at the end of their turn. If they do have more than nine, the player must gather them together and go to the banker and make a trade (for example, ten units for one long). Play does not proceed to the next player until all the trades have been made. The winner is the first player to earn five tens. This game can be modified by using two dice and increasing the winning amount.

The Take Away Game (Subtraction)

This game is simply the reverse of the Banker's Game. The emphasis here is on representing the regrouping of tens. Players must give back in units to the bank whatever is rolled on the die. To begin, all players place the same number of blocks on their boards. Exchanges must be made with the banker. Rules are quickly made by the students (for example, when rolling a six, a player may hand the banker a long and ask for four units back). It is helpful for students to explain their reasoning to one another. The winner is the first to have an empty playing board. Students should decide in their group, beforehand, regardless of whether an exact roll is necessary to go out.

Teaching Division with Understanding

Base-ten blocks bring understanding to an often complex algorithmic process. The following activity is a good place to start when introducing and representing division.

1. Using base-ten blocks, have students show 393 with flats, rods, and units.
2. Have the students divide the blocks into three equal piles.
3. Slowly ask students to explain what they did. How many flats in each pile, how many rods, and how many units?
4. Give students several more problems. Some examples: Start with 435, and divide into three piles. Encourage students to explain how many flats, rods, and units they found at the end of all their exchanges. In this problem, one flat will have to be exchanged for ten rods (tens) and then the rods divided into three groups. One rod remains. Next, students will have to exchange the one rod for ten units and then divide the units into three groups. No units are left in this problem. Continue doing more verbal problems, pausing, and letting students explain how they solved them. What exchanges were made? It is helpful to have students work together trying to explain their reasoning, correcting each other, and asking questions. (Burns, 1988)

5. After many problems, perhaps the next class session, explain to the students that they are now ready to record their work on paper, still using the blocks.

   a. The teacher then shows two ways to write the problem: $435 \div 3 =$ and $(435/3)$
   b. Then the teacher asks the students three questions and waits until all students have finished with each question.

   Question 1
   How many hundreds in each group? (Students go to their record sheet above the division symbol of the problem. They answer one flat, so they record "1" on their sheet.)
   Question 2
   How many in all? Students check how many cubes are represented; they answer "300," so they record "300" on their sheet.
   Question 3
   How many are left? Students return to the problem and perform this subtraction: $435 - 300 = 135$. Now the problem continues with the tens and then the ones. Again, they start over asking the three questions each time. (Burns, 1988)

6. For the advanced student, this seems like an elaborate way of doing division. By using manipulatives and teaching with understanding, beginning division makes sense to elementary students. Teachers can introduce shortcuts later to make more advanced division easier and faster.

Students learn best when they are actively engaged in meaningful mathematics tasks using hands-on materials. Such a mathematics classroom task encourages students' thinking, risk taking, and communicating with peers and adults about everyday experiences.

Sample Activities

In an effort to link the mathematics standards to classroom practice, a few sample activities are presented. The intent is not to prescribe an activity for a unique grade level, but rather to present activities that could be modified and used in many grades.

Activity: Estimate and Compare

Objectives: In grades K–4, the curriculum should include estimation so students can:

- explore estimation strategies.
- recognize when an estimate is appropriate.
- determine the reasonableness of results.
- apply estimation in working with quantities, measurement, computation, and problem solving.

Math and science instruction in the primary grades tries to make classifying and using numerals an essential part of classroom experience. Children need many opportunities to identify quantities and see relationships among objects. Students count and write numerals. When developing beginning concepts, students need to manipulate concrete materials and relate numbers to problem situations. They benefit by talking, writing, and hearing what others think. In the following activity, students are actively involved in estimating, manipulating objects, counting, verbalizing, writing, and comparing.

Directions

1. Divide students into small groups (two or three students). Place a similar group of objects in a color-coded container for each group. Pass out recording sheets divided into partitions with the color of the container in each box.
2. Have young students examine the container on their desks, estimate how many objects are present, discuss with their group, and write their guess next to the color on the sheet.
3. Next, have the group count the objects and write the number they counted next to the first number. Instruct the students to circle the greater number.
4. Switch cans or move to the next station and repeat the process. Different objects (small plastic cats, marbles, paper clips, colored shells, etc.) add interest and operate as a real motivator.

Activity: Adding and Subtracting in Real-Life Situations

Objectives: In early grades, the mathematics curriculum should include concepts of addition and subtraction of whole numbers so that students can develop meaning for the operations by modeling and discussing a variety of problem situations. Also, they should be able to relate the mathematical language and symbolism of operations to problem situations and informal language.

When students are learning about the operations of addition and subtraction, it is helpful for them to make connections between these processes and the world around them. Story problems using ideas from science help students see the actions of joining and separating. Using manipulatives and sample word problems gives students experience in joining sets and figuring out the differences between them. By pretending and using concrete materials, learning becomes more meaningful.

Directions

1. Divide students into small groups (two or three students).
2. Tell stories in which the learners can pretend to be animals, plants, other students, or even space creatures.
3. Telling stories is enhanced by having students use unifix cubes or other manipulatives to represent the people, objects, or animals in the oral problems.
4. Have students work on construction paper or prepare counting boards on which trees, oceans, trails, houses, space stations, and other things have been drawn.

Activity: Solving Problems

Problem solving should be the starting place for developing struggling students' understanding. Teachers should present word problems for students to discuss and find solutions working together, without the distraction of symbols. The following activities attempt to link word problems to meaningful situations.

Objectives: Students will:

- solve problems.
- work in a group.
- discuss and present their solutions.

Directions

1. Divide students into small groups (two or three students).

2. Find a creative way to share $50.00 among four students. Explain your solution. Is it fair? How could you do it differently?

3. The students in your class counted and found there were 163 sheets of construction paper. They were given the problem of figuring out how many sheets each child would receive if they were divided evenly among them.

4. Encourage students to explain their reasoning to the class.

5. After discussing each problem, show the students the standard notation for representing division. Soon you will find that students will begin to use the standard symbols in their own writing.

Activity: Using Statistics: Supermarket Shopping

Statistics is the science or study of data. Statistical problems require collecting, sorting, representing, analyzing, and interpreting information.

Objectives: Students will:

- collect, organize, and describe data.
- construct, read, and interpret displays of data.
- formulate and solve problems that involve collecting and analyzing data.

Problem

1. Your group has $20.00 to spend at the market. What will you purchase?

2. Have groups explain and write down their choices.

3. Next, have groups collect data from all the groups in the class.

4. Graph the class results.

Archimedes

Archimedes' inventions in ancient Greece planted the seeds that have grown into all kinds of modern technological innovations. The Archimedes screw, for example, is still being used to generate power. It does not have the capacity of a large hydropower dam, but it allows fish to swim through without much damage and can be adapted to provide enough electricity for a whole village.

Archimedes not only came up with new mathematical principles but also went on to solve physics problems and engineer devices that used his findings. Other citizens of Syracuse were encouraged to agree or disagree with his conception of the laws of nature, prove them mathematically, and go on to demonstrate an application.

An experimental example for young people:

Archimedes Principle. The law of buoyancy: The upward force on a submerged object equals the weight of the liquid displaced.

Activity: Water Pressure Experiment: What Will Float?

Purpose and Objectives: Through this activity, students will discover the effects of gravity and water pressure in a series of observations of objects that will or will not float.

Explain to the students that the weight of water gives it pressure. For an object to float, opposing forces work against each other. Gravity pulls down on the object, and the water pushes it up. If an object has a high volume and is light for its size, then it has a large surface area against which the water will push. Adding salt to the water will increase its density and make it more buoyant.

Archimedes came up with many lasting mathematical applications, including a moving planetarium and a mechanical claw that tipped Roman warships over. But the death ray he is said to have invented is a two-thousand-year-old myth.

What about the imaginative new technology of the twenty-first century?

> *[A]n underlying question looms, asking whether the Internet and the global supply chain have really accelerated ingenuity or merely sent us scurrying to build negligible novelties, soon to be forgotten.*
>
> —Jeff Blagdon, posted on theverge.com

The Interactive Future of Math Instruction

Instruction in mathematics has become much more than knowing how to balance a checkbook or estimating how long it will take to get to a new location. Over the last few decades, both teaching methods and subject matter content have changed. So have the textbooks. Teachers of mathematics no longer teach computation and procedures in isolation from the situations that require those skills. In today's schools, students learn to perform mathematics computations by working together to put these skills into practice (Cavanagh et al., 2004).

Over the last three decades, the term *arithmetic* has faded, while *mathematics inquiry*, *mathematical reasoning*, and *problem solving* have moved front and center. Whether it is asking questions, gathering evidence, making conjectures, formulating models, or building sound arguments, this is mathematics today. As the National Council of Teachers of Mathematics' most recent guidelines point out, basic arithmetic skills must not be neglected. Problem solving and inquiry may be the keys to mathematics instruction in the twenty-first century, but computational skills like addition, subtraction, multiplication, division, fractions, and mental arithmetic still provide the foundation.

To help their students achieve a deeper understanding, more attention is being given to application and social interaction. Collaborative inquiry and problem-solving activities have become important up-to-date routes to deep knowledge in mathematics. Now students must be able to use a wide range of mathematical tools to solve math-related problems.

Knowing mathematics means being able to use it in purposeful ways. It also means being able to understand the role that mathematics serves in society.

NEW IDEAS ON TEACHING AND LEARNING

There is general agreement that a constructive, active view of learning must be reflected in the way that math and science are taught (Van De Walle, 2004). Classroom mathematics experiences should stimulate students, build on past understandings, and explore their own ideas. This means that students have many chances to interpret math ideas and construct understandings for themselves.

Reluctant learners need to be involved in problem-solving investigations and projects that engage thinking and reasoning. Working with materials in a group situation helps reinforce thinking. Students talk together, present their understandings, and try to make sense of the task.

Some of the newest methods for teaching mathematics in active small-group situations include writing about how they solved problems, keeping daily logs or journals, and expressing attitudes through creative endeavors such as building or artwork.

With the renewed emphasis on thinking, communicating, and making connections between topics, students are more in control of their learning. With collaborative inquiry, students have many experiences with manipulatives, calculators, computers, and working on real-world applications.

There are more opportunities to make connections and work with peers on interesting problems. The ability to express basic math understandings, to estimate confidently, and check the reasonableness of their estimates is part of what it means to be literate, numerate, and employable.

Whether it is making sense of newspaper graphs, identifying the dangers of global warming, or reading schedules at work, mathematics has real meaning in our lives. The same might be said for using the calculator, working with paper and pencil, or doing mental mathematics. Students must also master the basic facts of arithmetic before they can harness the full power of mathematics.

Unfortunately, simply learning to do algorithms (the step-by-step procedures used to compute with numbers) will not ensure success with problems that demand reasoning ability. The good news is that the curriculum is changing to make mathematics more interactive and relevant to what students need to know in order to meet changing intellectual and societal demands. And it is doing this without dropping the underlying structure of mathematics.

Teachers have found that the more opportunities students have to participate with others, the more likely they are to learn to do mathematics in knowledgeable and meaningful ways.

Quite simply, struggling students learn more if they have opportunities to describe their own ideas, listen to others, and cooperatively solve problems. All collaborative or cooperative learning structures are designed to increase student participation in learning, while building on the twin incentives of shared group goals and individual accountability.

Building teamwork skills, creative thinking, intellectual curiosity, and refining the emotions all have roles to play in developing motivation, knowledge, and new ideas. When failure occurs, remember the old saying: Genius is the ability to make all the possible mistakes in the least amount of time.

Teaching, Learning, and Understanding Mathematics

- Introduce math concepts in real-world settings.
- Develop an understanding of the math operations (adding, subtracting, multiplying, dividing) by tapping into students' curiosity.
- Use differentiated instruction to allow for students' learning styles.
- Integrate ideas with the mathematics standards.
- Plan stimulating lessons.

- Adapt textbook materials to reflect student interest.
- Let learners explore materials before they use them.
- Design a rubric or rating scale to assess student performance.

A simple rubric is an overall rating scale from 1 (needs additional instruction) to 4 (exemplary).

Peer support helps students feel more confident and willing to make mistakes that go hand in hand with serious inquiry. So regardless of whether you want to paint it in the subtle hues of collaborative inquiry or the day-glow colors of cooperative learning, student learning teams are a powerful way to approach mathematics instruction for reluctant math students.

What about teacher directions? The best approach is often telling students *what* to do but not *how* to do it. Many students are finely tuned to come up with the answers the teacher wants. So when it comes to mathematical problem solving, it is more interesting to solve problems for which there is not an obvious answer.

Learning, like math and science, has a lot to do the ability to change our minds. Dead ends, false starts, and danger go with the territory. Take the example of big data. It has its scary aspects and obvious limitations. It also has some useful qualities in areas like medicine and city planning. But what do new sources of data, like huge secret stockpiles of telephone records and personal e-mails, have to say about us?

Students bring to school all kinds of media experiences that shape their understanding of mathematics and life. Therefore, it makes sense for teachers to encourage students to explore some of the math concepts (like probability and graphs) that are viewed and read on the screen every day (Chappell and Thompson, 2009).

PROBLEMS AND OPPORTUNITIES IN A NUMERICAL AGE

We live in an era when people and things are observed and subject to the numerical imagination. Whether data is collected by the school, business, or government, the fact is that there are many important things that are either difficult or impossible to measure. There are dimensions of reality and truth that go well beyond anything in the data.

Some of the new tools brought to us by mathematical algorithms and the Internet may actually boost learning. But others lend themselves to distraction and inquiries into trivia. Can social networks serve as a good place for collaborative learning? Maybe. But the notion of harnessing the collective creativity of users can be lost in the quest for Facebook "likes."

Applying mathematical algorithms to big data (metadata) has all kinds of possibilities—including social engineering. Facebook, for example, uses such math tools to find those who are most likely to share certain kinds of experiences with others. Once a large amount of data is built up, personal information can be shared with those who may have similar interests. This creates new social arrangements and the sharing of even more information.

Social networks often result in privacy falling by the wayside. There are, however, different levels of privacy protection, just as there are different levels of cloud computing through which you go online to store data or retrieve an app.

Although they may be controlled by digital devices, not all new technologies are digital at their core.

It may seem counterintuitive, but more advanced technologies may actually be able to help solve some of the problems generated by what is around today. For example, global warming and environmental pollution were made worse by older technologies like coal-burning power plants. Newer technologies like wind power and solar panels can actually help mitigate some of the effects.

The on-rushing technological future represents both the problems and the opportunities confronting a twenty-first-century world. Dealing with today's challenges requires developing a broad educational and political will.

A good place to start is dealing with personal well-being and privacy on the Internet. It may be a borderless space, but much of the infrastructure is in the United States. Also, America's National Security Administration (NSA) has eavesdropping posts around the world to gather information. The next step is using mathematical tools (algorithms) to sort through an enormous volume of stored metadata on phone calls, e-mails, books purchased online, and just about everything else.

There are both business and governmental dimensions when it comes to the gathering of information or conducting surveillance. For firms like Facebook, Google, and Microsoft, the motive is profit. Governmental examples include the NSA effort to gather just about every electronically based conversation on earth—and then use mathematical algorithms to predict behavior.

Streams of information are easy to collect when the bits are "in motion." When it is "at rest" in a server or elsewhere, the government goes to Internet and telephone companies and gets it. This brings up an interesting question:

Whom do you trust more with your personal information—the government or the commercial world? Do you trust one, both, or neither? Should you know when you are being examined?

The Internet increasingly augments the way we collaborate, think, and learn. It is part of our lives. Big data, big surveillance, and cloud computing are all part of the same package; they have become an inescapable part of the personal, commercial, and economic environment. A major problem is that the technical frameworks were put into place before much thought was given to establishing a level of protection for either the data or the consumer.

In this age of metadata, rapid automation, and globalization, we have to work smarter, harder, and bring innovation to whatever we do. Continuous critical thinking, learning, and retooling are now the norm. In a world filled with the technology applications of mathematical inquiry, knowing about math and its associates is more important than ever.

Students need to explore and have some understanding of the many ways that math and its associates impact their day-to-day lives. Being afraid, naive, or uninformed about basic arithmetic, mathematics, and related technological products can be a real problem at school, in the workplace, and for citizens in a democracy.

Asking the schools to do more is reasonable, but asking them to solve the nation's social and educational problems on their own is not.

SUMMARY, CONCLUSION, AND LOOKING AHEAD

Difficulties in math can lead to all kinds of misconceptions and general underachievement across the curriculum (Leinwand, 2012). Just as with print literacy, without a sense of mathematical ways of thinking (numeracy), there are many important things that a student simply will not be able to do.

Mathematics has been called the language of nature. A better understanding of this language can be facilitated by exploring math-related problems. Such investigations and collaborative activities are likely to be interesting for all students—especially reluctant learners.

The National Council of Teachers of Mathematics and the Mathematical Sciences Education Board suggest changes in what mathematics we teach, how it is taught, and how to get all learners involved. The Common Core standards take a similar approach.

An understanding of concepts, proficiency with skills, and a positive attitude all have roles to play in mathematical literacy. Seeing math as part of the wider world, rather than simply dry problems or dull textbooks, is crucial for getting all students involved.

We are living an age of numerical data. Thus, it is important to go beyond test results to a wider array of data, thus allowing us to take a personalized look at each student.

In the classroom, meeting the needs of learners from an increasingly wide range of cultures and backgrounds requires active learning techniques. Also, learning to deal with diversity can actually be a positive factor when it comes to preparing young people for life in a global society.

As students work together to gain mathematical reasoning skills, they are more likely to have a positive attitude toward each other and toward math (O'Connell and SanGiovanni, 2013). Building competency and confidence together is bound to have a positive effect students' willingness to learn math content.

Much of what we do in the future will be based on the best of today's commonsense and classroom-proven approaches that work for teachers at any grade level. Differentiated instruction and collaborative problem solving are good examples. Both are particularly helpful for teachers who are trying to provide struggling students with experiences that can enable them to acquire mathematical knowledge.

Mathematics is more than a language for describing the natural world. It can also use visual media to describe common events in everyday life—as well as complex events in science, technology, business, and just about everything else. Graphics and media images can also be very useful in stimulating mathematical conversations that are centered around the Common Core State Standards (Small, 2013).

The mathematics curriculum is continually changing to reflect the needs of students with diverse learning needs. A math-rich classroom environment might include student work samples, number lines, and even a math literature collection (Moynihan, 2012). The diversity of today's students requires a differentiated approach to instruction in order to meet student needs, societal demands, and the math application needs of today and tomorrow.

The future is not preordained. Changes come about because as the possible alternatives are worked on today and tomorrow, someone cooperatively struggles to make it happen. For the best outcomes, it is important for individuals to go beyond technical skills and build on qualities like critical thinking, intellectual curiosity, and collaborating with a wide range of people.

As teachers go about matching math instruction to the readiness, interests, and talents of all students, the result is likely to be the development of a natural sense of community in the classroom. This can help provide social support for recognizing the relationship of mathematical problems to life outside of school.

The major goal of mathematics education is helping students become mathematically empowered. In a math-rich classroom environment, learners can gain confidence in their ability to understand and apply math. Hopefully, along the way they will also develop an appreciation of the power, beauty, and fascination of mathematics.

Numeracy is to mathematics as literacy is to language.

—L. Steen

QUESTIONS FOR TEACHERS AND PROSPECTIVE TEACHERS

1. What have you done recently that is unique and somehow related to mathematics?
2. What real-world experience could a teacher use to engage students in a discussion about understanding math operations (adding, subtracting, multiplying, dividing)? Design a computation task that engages students' interests and intellect.
3. What role do culture, attitude, engagement, and math knowledge play in gaining an imaginative understanding of the implications of mathematics and its technological products?
4. Design a question or activity that focuses on estimation and problem solving in a way that promotes the investigation and growth of mathematical ideas.
5. How would you focus on helping struggling or reluctant learners make sense of mathematics and see the subject in a more positive light?
6. The attitude of fear and dislike of math are often related. Design a math lesson that involves collaborative reasoning in a way that is somehow intrinsically interesting, surprising, and aesthetically pleasing.

REFERENCES AND RESOURCES

Bender, W. (2013). *Differentiating Math Instruction, K–8: Common Core Mathematics in the 21st Century Classroom.* 3rd ed. Thousand Oaks, CA: Corwin/SAGE.

Benjamin, A. (2003). *Differentiated Instruction: A Guide for Elementary School Teachers.* Larchmont, NY: Eye On Education.

Burns, M. (2004). "Ten Big Math Ideas by Marilyn Burns." *Instructor* 113 (7): 16–19.

Burns, M. (1988). *Mathematics with Manipulatives.* (Six videos). White Plains, NY: Cuisinaire Company of America.

Burns, M. (2001). *About Teaching Mathematics: A K–8 Resource.* White Plains, NY: Math Solutions.

Cathcart, W. G., Pothier, Y., Vance, J., & Bezuk, N. (2010). *Learning Mathematics in Elementary and Middle Schools: A Learner-centered Approach.* 5th ed. Upper Saddle River, NJ: Pearson Education.

Cavanagh, M., Dacey, L., Findell, C., Greenes, C., Sheffield, L., & Small, M. (2004). *Navigating Through Number and Operations in Prekindergarten–Grade 2.* Reston, VA: National Council of Teachers of Mathematics.

Chappell, M., & Thompson, D. (2009). *Math, Culture, and Popular Media.* Portsmouth, NH: Heinemann.

Empson, S., & Levi, L. (2011). *Extending Childrens' Mathematics: Fractions and Decimals.* Portsmouth, NH: Heinemann.

House, P. (2013). *What's So Funny About Math?* Reston, VA: National Council of Teachers of Mathematics.

Leinwand, S. (2012). *Sensible Mathematics: A Guide for School Leaders in the Era of Common Core.* 2nd ed. Portsmouth, NH: Heinemann.

Marzano, R., & Simms, J. (2013). *Vocabulary for the Common Core.* Alexandria, VA: Association for Supervision and Curriculum Development.

Moynihan, C. (2012). *Math Sense: The Look, Sound, and Feel of Effective Instruction.* Portland, ME: Stenhouse Publishers.

National Council of Teachers of Mathematics (NCTM). (2000). *Principles and Standards for School Mathematics.* Reston, VA: National Council of Teachers of Mathematics.

O'Connell, S., & SanGiovanni, J. (2013). *Putting the Best Practices into Action: Implementing the Common Core Standards for Mathematical Practice K–8.* Portsmouth, NH: Heinemann.

Paulos, J. (1988). *Innumeracy: Mathematical Illiteracy and Its Consequences.* New York, NY: Farrar, Straus, and Giroux.

Polya, G. (1957). *How to Solve It.* 2nd ed. Princeton, NJ: Princeton University Press.

Ripley, A. (2013). *The Smartest Kids in the World—and How They Got that Way.* New York, NY: Simon & Schuster.

Small, M. (2013). *Eyes on Math: A Visual Approach to Teaching Math Concepts.* New York, NY: Teachers College Press.

Steen, L. (1990). "Numeracy." *Daedalus* 119 (2): 211–231.

Van De Walle, J. (2004). *Elementary and Middle School Mathematics: Thinking Developmentally.* 5th ed. Boston, MA: Pearson Education.

Chapter Four

Science Involving All Students with Active Involvement and Collaborative Inquiry

Curiosity is the engine of achievement.

—Ken Robinson

Science is an exciting and interesting system of knowing about the world and beyond. Scientific knowledge is based on information and knowledge built up by observation, experimentation, and collaborative inquiry. Intellectual curiosity is a key human variable. Since scientists usually do their work in association with others, it is best if students learn science in a similar fashion.

When it comes to student achievement, the difference makers are knowledgeable teachers who encourage creative inquiry and spark the imaginations of young people. So it is up to educators to build up their ideas about pedagogy and science education in ways that allow them to make informed choices.

As seasoned teachers know, it is best not to assume that one student's optimum path for learning is identical to that of another student.

In the classroom, it helps if teachers differentiate by using a variety of classroom practices that closely attend to students' prior knowledge, learning styles, and social comfort zones. The next step is activating the social nature of learning as students collaboratively move toward scientific literacy and the skills they need to make sound societal decisions (Wickman, 2013).

It is a good idea to connect the scientific processes and related inquiry skills to many aspects of classroom life. Later in this chapter, you will find a sampling of active learning activities designed to help teachers open up possibilities for students that cut across subject matter boundaries to get at the big ideas of science.

Since there can be no intelligent inquiry in a vacuum, teachers have to provide information, generate excitement, and suggest questioning possibilities. From time to time, a little coaching helps. And yes, even lower-grade children can be encouraged to ask their own big questions.

At every grade level, science instruction is built on the teacher's knowledge about the nature of the subject. In addition, an understanding of how students should go about the process of scientific inquiry certainly helps. Of course, this is asking a lot when elementary school teachers frequently have to teach dozens of subjects.

Even if science instruction is not playing to their strength, teachers must have a firm grasp of the characteristics of effective instruction. And whatever their subject matter background, it is important for educators to realize that attitude and enthusiasm matter for everyone involved.

Students' attitudes influence their level of achievement. And a positive disposition also goes hand in hand with learning scientific principles and processes.

When it comes to motivating students, collaborative inquiry is something most teachers know and like. It can play a major role across the curriculum. The cooperative process involves having students work with one, two, or three others as they build on their own curiosity, pose questions, and actively seek answers.

The observing, measuring, collecting, and classifying parts of science come naturally to many students. But it is a pain for others. Working in small groups in which the other students have a positive attitude helps even the most reluctant learner. To improve teamwork skills, the teacher could ask students, at the end of their group work, to discuss what could be done to improve the process next time

Having some idea about the impact of the technological tools of science is an important element in science instruction today. Digital devices are getting smaller and faster, with high-resolution graphics, simulation, and virtual reality, all presenting additional possibilities for joining with and enhancing student understanding of the natural world. In fact, some online experiences are beginning to approach those of real life.

An important goal of science education is to open the minds of all students in a way that expands their perception and appreciation of the very nature of life—water, rocks, plants, animals, people, and other elements of the world. The Next Generation Science Standards (NGSS Lead States, 2013) support the use of technology and collaborative inquiry and recommend ways to get all students more excited about science.

Experience, practical wisdom, and a little rule bending have roles to play in both creativity and quality instruction. The same can be said for cultivating students' imagination and acknowledging multiple types of intelligence. Experienced teachers can help by mentoring new teachers as they work to become more effective, spontaneous, and creative.

When all is said and done, it is up to individual teachers to discover how science instruction can enhance the curiosity, interest, and scientific knowledge of all students.

THE EMERGING SCIENCE CURRICULUM

To paraphrase the National Science Education Standards, "Science teaching is at its best in classrooms that are communities in which all students learn science through inquiry and active involvement."

The past quarter-century has seen several successful efforts to alter the goals of science education and change how the subject is taught. There is ever-increasing emphasis on inquiry and imaginative problem solving. Also, digital technology is getting more important.

The past is never fully the past—and the future is never fully the future. In the classroom, there are certain constants like the need for scientific reasoning and learning how to learn.

The technological products of science have sparked changes in the practices of working scientists, the economy, and how people live and work. Technology shapes culture and culture returns the favor. At a personal level, a student's social culture shapes many things. Still, what happens at school can make a big difference.

Along their way to scientific literacy, students can learn that the organizing principles of science apply to local *and* global phenomena. Globalization, for example, is both useful and problematic. Some countries, like France, view globalization as Americanization. Who is helped by outsourcing? Is globalization a way to produce inexpensive products or a rush to the bottom in wages and working conditions?

Whatever your view of current events, other countries are quickly moving up the educational competency ladder while the United States stays about the same. We have only started to realize the new conditions in an interconnected world. The competitive educational and economic situation is the good, the bad, and the worrisome. But however you view new national realities, all of our students need access to quality science classes if they are to achieve higher levels of scientific understanding.

Culture, education, and just about everything else are now being influenced by a global economy, information technology, differing family structures, and a society that is knowledge intensive. All of these affect the world of education, work, and how we think about learning.

Home environment, health, economics, and teamwork skills influence different levels of student achievement. Educational success also has a lot to do with what happens to teachers and students in classrooms. No matter what takes place outside of school, the sparks of good teaching can implant knowledge deeply into student memory.

An active participatory science curriculum has the power to make a difference in the lives of all students and in the society where they live. In such an environment, it is important to provide ways for all students, including those who struggle with science and math, to learn content as deeply and quickly as possible. And this must be done without hindering high-achieving students.

A modern science curriculum has the following:

1. Greater depth and less superficial coverage
2. A focus on inquiry and problem solving
3. Attention to skills and knowledge of the subject
4. Provision for individual differences and collaboration
5. A common core of subject matter
6. Close coordination to related subjects such as mathematics
7. Connection to an integrated curriculum
8. Personal relevance for students

In the last century, extensive science education often did not begin until middle or high school. The new guidelines call for injecting more science instruction into the primary and middle grades. Even the realities of climate change and natural selection are now considered appropriate topics at all grade levels.

Respecting student individual differences, modern science instruction provides help for those students who are having difficulties. Learners may have many ways of displaying and transferring knowledge. Therefore, seasoned teachers often go beyond the verbal and add visual representations. Examples include directional charts (similar to a road map) and web diagrams with main ideas in the middle and spokes going out to subtopics.

Teachers may provide a scaffolding structure and offer suggestions, cues, and explanations. Such an approach recognizes multiple intelligences and is designed to accommodate individual differences. When teachers realize that one size does not fit all, they can make a big difference—especially when attending to the differing social and academic needs of diverse learners.

To paraphrase Vygotsky, as collaborative lessons and projects progress, students will be more able to creatively solve problems *together today*. And they will be just as able to solve problems *alone tomorrow* (Dixon-Krauss, 1996).

Active Learning, Content Integration, and the Standards

Another characteristic of today's science curriculum is that it is closely coordinated with related subjects. This is especially true of two tools of science: mathematics and technology. The mathematics curriculum, for example, often supports and connects to the science curriculum.

Instead of being taught as a separate subject, science is included by many K–8 schools as part of an integrated curriculum. Integration results in better achievement and improved attitudes. Science-related disciplines like biology, chemistry, earth science, engineering, and physics all have at least minor roles to play at every grade level.

The most important change in science education is in the nature of science itself. Some of the sciences now go beyond theories and events related to the natural world to deal with personal and social problems. There is much greater uncertainty when you have to deal with complex and unique human beings.

Physics and chemistry are good examples of hard sciences. The behavioral sciences are different. But when it comes to fields like education and psychology, there is a recognized need to go beyond empirical knowledge and into the realm of improvisation and artistry.

A quality science curriculum needs to be teacher friendly, with clear objectives and activities that support inquiry. Teaching requires a combination of technical expertise and personal knowledge. So teachers need to have one foot in science and the other foot in the liberal arts.

For both teacher and student, personal relevance and technology are tools that have proven to be beneficial when it comes to learning science. Overall, motivation is enhanced and science lessons are made more meaningful when inquiry touches on real-life situations and actual problems.

The Next Generation Science Standards (NGSS), a National Academies of Science publication, came out in 2013. This framework builds on past standards efforts. *A Framework for K–12 Science Education*, from the National Research Council, is another source of influence in modern science education (NRC, 2012).

Suggestions for science education are as follows:

- Include engineering and scientific thinking. The basic idea is to provide students with many chances to gain an understanding of the nature of science and core ideas behind science practices.
- Teaching practices, including process skills, need to be taught along with science content. In the past, process skills were often missing.
- Use cross-cutting ideas (like themes) in constructing understanding.
- Employ continuous progressions.

Developing the ability to think critically and creatively is key to becoming continuing learners who can apply knowledge in the local and global community.

Today's science curriculum offers a common core of subject matter that is designed to draw students together. This is in contrast to yesterday's fragmented curriculum, which separated students according to ability or career goals. The basic idea today is to provide access to every student. This is done by meeting the needs of those who require extra help while also providing special enrichment for those who have advanced beyond their peers.

Scientific inquiry has a lot to do with exploring the different ways that scientists study the natural world and explain what they find based on the solid evidence. To have a better chance of reaching all students, it is best to minimize the learning aggravations and maximize the opportunity to participate in a skill-oriented inquiry science program.

It helps if the teacher is aware of a student's past learning experience and is capable of looking ahead to future possibilities. Another key to success is responding to individual differences in ways that assist learners in building collaborative unity and developing moral character.

Strategies for Helping All Students

Science can be the most exciting experience for elementary and middle-school students and teachers if it is taught as an active, hands-on subject in which students learn by doing.

Many strategies are based on the idea that teachers adapt instruction to student differences (Benjamin, 2003). Today, teachers are determined to reach all students, trying to provide the right level of challenge for students who perform below grade level, for gifted students, and for everyone in between. They are working to deliver instruction in ways that meet the needs of auditory, visual, and kinesthetic learners, while trying to connect to students' personal interests. (See the strategies below.)

1. Use a Collaborative Approach

Collaborative learning is a "total class" approach that lends itself to students who are having difficulties. It requires everyone to think, learn, and teach others. Within a cooperative learning classroom, there will be many and varied strengths among students. Every student will possess characteristics that will lend themselves to enriching learning for all their peers.

Sometimes "differences" may constitute a conventionally defined "disability," and sometimes it simply means the inability to do a certain life or school-related task. Other times it means (as with the academically talented) being capable of work well beyond the norm. Within the collaborative learning classroom, such exceptionality need not constitute a handicap.

Collaborative learning that is inclusive of all students is not simply a technique that a teacher can just select and adopt in order to "accommodate" a student with a disability within the regular classroom. Making changes in the classroom process may require that teachers undergo changes in the ways that they teach and in the ways they view students. This means creating comfortable, yet challenging, learning environments rich in diversity. The goal is collaboration among all types of learners. In mixed-ability groups, the emphasis must be on proficiency rather than age or grade level as the basis for student progress.

Active collaboration requires a depth of planning and a redefinition of planning, testing, and classroom management. Perhaps most significantly, collaborative learning values individual abilities, talents, skills, and background knowledge. In a collaborative learning classroom, conventionally defined "disabilities" fade into the heterogeneity of expected and anticipated differences among all students.

2. Form Multi-Age Flexible Groups

Schools have tried to meet the needs of struggling and advanced learners by pulling them out of regular classrooms. This has resulted in many problems. Struggling students will experience more long-term success by being placed in heterogeneous classes. In these classes, success is more likely only if teachers are ready and able to meet them at their point of readiness and systematically escalate their learning until they are able to function as competently and confidently as other learners.

To maximize the potential of each learner, educators need to meet each student at his or her starting point and ensure substantial growth during each school term. Classrooms that respond to student differences benefit virtually all students. Being flexible in grouping students gives students many options to develop their particular strengths and show their performance (Tomlinson and Cunningham Eidson, 2003).

3. Set Up Learning Centers

A learning center is a space in the class that contains a group of activities or materials designed to teach, reinforce, or extend a particular concept. Centers generally focus on an important topic and use materials and activities addressing a wide range of reading levels, learning profiles, and student interests.

A teacher may create many centers such as a science center, a music center, or a reading center. Students do not need to move to all of them at once to achieve competence with a topic or a set of skills. Teachers should have students rotate among the centers. Learning centers generally include simple to complex activities.

Effective learning centers usually provide clear directions for students including what students should do if they complete a task or what to do if they need help. A record-keeping system should be there to monitor what students do at the center. An ongoing assessment of student growth in the class should be in place, which can lead to teacher adjustments in center tasks.

4. Develop Tiered Activities

These are helpful strategies when teachers want to address students with different learning needs. For example, a student who struggles with reading from a science textbook or has a difficult time with complex vocabulary needs some help in trying to make sense of the important ideas in a given chapter. At the same time, a student who is advanced well beyond grade level needs to find a genuine challenge in working with the same concepts.

Teachers use tiered activities so that all students focus on necessary understandings and skills, albeit at different levels of complexity and abstractness. By keeping the focus of the activities the same but providing different routes of access, the teacher maximizes the likelihood that each student will come away with important skills and be appropriately challenged.

Teachers should select the concepts and skills that will be the focus of the activity for all learners. Using assessments to find out what the students need and creating interesting activities that will cause learners to use an important skill or understand a key idea are examples of the tiered approach.

Teachers should think about, or actually draw, a ladder that places the student on a skill level (the top step represents learners with very high skills, the bottom step is for learners with low skills and poor understanding of complex concepts). It is important to provide varying materials and activities. Teachers match a version of the task to each student based on student needs and task requirements. The goal is to match the task's degree of difficulty and the students' level of readiness.

5. Make Learning More Challenging

Research indicates that alternative strategies that address the causes of poor performance offer hope for helping students succeed. Challenging strategies put more emphasis on authentic "real-world" problems, in which students are encouraged to formulate their own problems on a topic they are interested in and work together to solve it. Teachers should allow time for student discussions and sharing of ideas.

6. Have a Clear Set of Standards

Integrating standards into the curriculum helps make learning more meaningful and interesting to reluctant students. Having a clearly defined set of standards helps teachers concentrate on instruction and makes the expectations of the class clear to students. Students come to understand what is expected and work collaboratively to achieve it.

Challenging groups to help each group member succeed is a good way to avoid poor performance by reluctant learners. Competition, anxiety, and lack of problem-solving abilities have been identified as problems that prevent achievement.

7. Expand Learning Options

Not all students learn in the same way or at the same time. Teachers can expand learning options by differentiating instruction. This means teachers should reach out to struggling students or small groups to create the best learning experience possible (Tomlinson and Cunningham Eidson, 2003).

8. Introduce Active Reading Strategies

There is an approach that uses "active reading" strategies to improve students' abilities to explain difficult text. This step-by-step process involves reading aloud to yourself or someone else as a way to build science understandings.

Although most learners self-explain without verbalizing, the active reading approach is similar to that used by anyone attempting to master new material: the best way to truly learn is to teach by explaining something to someone else.

Find and use some quotes. For example, what did American inventor Thomas Edison mean when he said, "Because I readily absorb ideas from every source—frequently starting where the last person left off—I am sometimes accurately described as more of a sponge than an inventor" (de Mauro, 2005)?

Another thoughtful quote is as follows: "Generations before us were so amazed by the electric light, the telegraph, and the radio that they thought they had arrived at the zenith of human achievement" (Morozov, 2013). Are we in danger of making the same mistake?

Students in the upper grades might enjoy speculating about the nature of the universe. If the parameters of our universe differed by more than a little, the complex molecules needed for life would not have formed. How did the Big Bang get it just right? Was there a type of natural selection at work when the universe got started? What is the role of black energy (that pervades the universe) and black holes? Did the existence of black holes also depend getting the strength of nuclear forces right for life?

It is important to learn that there are many open questions in science. And fifth graders can speculate with the best of them. Using the Large Hadron Collider and images from space, scientists have conducted experiments and observations that trace things back to the first few seconds of the universe. But who knows what it was like before the Big Bang—or how things worked out like they did (Smolin, 2013)?

THE CHANGING SCIENCE CURRICULUM

Today, active science learning in the elementary and middle schools is changing the traditional textbook process. It contributes to the development of interdisciplinary skills. For example, the overlap in science and mathematics is obvious when one looks at suggestions for skill development in both subjects.

Many of the best models in science education involve having students work in cross-subject and mixed-ability teams. Teachers begin by making connections among science, mathematics, and real-world concerns (a good example would be those found in the newspaper). The live action of science education and literacy is in the hands of teachers.

To use and understand science today requires an awareness of what the scientific endeavor is and how it relates to our culture and our lives. The National Council on Science and Technology Education identifies a scientifically literate person as one who recognizes the diversity and unity of the natural world, understands the important concepts and principles of science, and is aware of the ways that science, mathematics, and technology depend on each other.

> *Scientific literacy implies that a person can identify scientific issues underlying national and local decisions and express positions that are scientifically and technologically informed.*
> —National Science Education Standards

Reviewing the National Science Content Standards

The classroom must be the focus of the Science Education Standards. The content standards outline what students should know, understand, and be able to do. The standards are described as follows:

- Linking the science ideas and process skills
- Applying science as inquiry
- Becoming aware of physical, life, earth, and space science through activity-based learning
- Using science understandings to design solutions to problems
- Understanding the connection of science and technology
- Examining and practicing science from personal and social viewpoints
- Discovering the history and nature of science through readings, discussions, observations, and writings (National Research Council, 2000)

Science Inquiry and Process Skills

The inquiry skills of science are acquired through a questioning process. As we discussed in chapter 2, this question about inquiry directs the searcher to knowledge, whether newly discovered by the individual or new ideas not yet explored in the field. Inquiry also raises new questions and directions for examination. The findings may generate ideas or suggest connections or ways of expressing concepts and interrelationships more clearly.

The process of inquiry helps struggling students grow in content knowledge and the processes and skills of the search. It also invites reluctant learners to explore anything that interests them. Whatever the problem, subject, or issue, any inquiry that is done with enthusiasm and with care will use some of the same thinking processes that are utilized by scholars who are searching for new knowledge in their field of study.

Inquiry processes form a foundation of understanding and are components of the basic goals and standards of science and mathematics. These goals are intertwined and multidisciplinary, providing students many opportunities to become involved in inquiry. Each goal involves one or more processes (or investigations). The emphasis clearly has shifted from content toward *process*.

STANDARDS-BASED SCIENCE ACTIVITIES

Activity 1: Mystery Liquids: Experiment

Inquiry Skills: hypothesizing, experimenting, and communicating.

Science Standards: inquiry, physical science, science and technology, personal perspectives, written communications.

Directions

In this exploring activity, students are experimenting with chemicals and doing physical science work. They are learning to use tools found in the lab and becoming familiar with the safety rules of science, mathematics, and technology. Review with the students the properties of matter (solids and liquids), and then present them with the mystery compound (made from cornstarch and water).

Background Information
Facts about solids:

- do not change shape easily
- will not allow another solid to pass through it easily
- are usually visible
- have a definite shape
- when heated become liquid
- when cooled stay solid

Facts about liquids:

- change shapes easily (take the shape of the container)
- will allow a solid to pass through easily
- may be visible or invisible
- have a definite shape
- when heated become gas
- when cooled become solid

Introduce the activity by talking about liquids and define the characteristics of a liquid. Have students think of all the liquids they encounter every day. Present the problem and the rules to the class.

Problem: Have students try to find out what the four mystery liquids are.

Rules

1. Each liquid is a household substance that may or may not have been colored with food coloring to hide its identity.
2. Students are limited to using only their sense of sight to do this experiment. Absolutely no tasting or touching the liquids! *Students should experiment by manipulating.*

3. For safety reasons, caution students they are NOT TO SMELL, TOUCH, OR TASTE the chemicals.
4. Each medicine dropper may be used to pick up only one liquid. We do not want contamination!

Purpose

Students will experiment with a cornstarch and water mixture trying to discover some of the properties of the magic mixture. Students will perform a variety of experiments to answer if the magic compound is a solid or a liquid.

Materials for Each Table

- 5 plastic containers
- 5 liquids (oil, water, soap, alcohol, vinegar)
- 5 medicine droppers
- 2 beakers, 1 large and 1 small
- 1 tray
- 1 sheet each of plastic wrap, aluminum foil, and waxed paper
- 1 box of cornstarch
- 1 cup of water
- 1 aluminum pie tin
- 2 paper cups
- student worksheets or science/math journal

Procedures

1. Set up the containers with liquids.
2. Discuss the colored liquids.
3. Set up the trays with papers and materials for each group (5 eye droppers, 2 beakers, 1 small plastic container).

Background Information

To make the mystery compound, mix 1 box of cornstarch with 1 cup of water. Food coloring can be added if you choose. The mystery matter mixture has properties of both a solid and a liquid. Students make a prediction about the mystery matter mixture, record their observations, and then use data to support that prediction.

Procedure

1. Review the properties of matter. Ask this question: "Is the mystery matter a solid or a liquid?"
2. Pass out materials, and allow students to "play" with the substance for a few minutes and record their observations.
3. Have students conduct the experiments with the mystery compound and record their results on their worksheets or in their science/math journal.
4. Instruct students to analyze their data, answer the question, and support their conclusion.

Data (Observation) Sheet

1. Color
2. Texture (What does it look and feel like?)
3. What is its shape?

Experiment: Do Each Test. Record Your Results.

1. The quick finger-poke test: Have students try to poke their finger into the mystery matter so that the tip of their finger touches the bottom of the pan. In order to make sure that this is the *quick* finger-poke test, try to touch the bottom of the pan in 1 second. (Like your finger is touching a hot stove!)
2. The slow finger-poke test: Have students try to poke their finger into the mystery matter so that the tip of their finger touches the bottom of the pan. In order to make sure that this is the *slow* finger-poke test, try to touch the bottom of the pan in 10 seconds. (Like your finger is moving in slow motion.)
3. Shape test: Put some mystery matter into one paper cup. Check to see if the mystery matter takes the shape of the cup or if it stays in its first shape.
4. Pour test: Try to pour the mystery matter from one cup to another.
5. Bounce test: Hold the mystery matter about 12 inches from the desk. Drop the mystery matter. Does it bounce?
6. Ball test: Have students try to form the mystery matter into a ball. Check to see if it holds its shape for 5 seconds.

7. Heat test: Let the teacher know when your group gets to this point. The teacher will do this experiment for your group, or your group may wish to try it with teacher supervision. Make a container out of foil. Fashion a bump on one side to clip on a clothes pin. Put a small amount of the mystery matter in the container over a votive candle.
8. Cool test (after heat test): Let the mystery matter cool to room temperature.
9. Shatter test: The teacher will do this experiment for the group, or the group may choose to try it with teacher supervision. Have students put the mystery matter in waxed paper on the table see if they can shatter it with the hammer.

Results

1. Encourage students to write a description of the activity.
2. Explain how the group went about solving the problem.
3. Record each experiment on a pie graph stating the chemical and your guesses.

Evaluation

1. Share the results.
2. Write about what the group learned from the activity.
3. Give some follow-up suggestions of how the activity could be improved. Encourage struggling students to work with their group and follow the procedures.

Follow-Up
Have students work together to write answers to these questions:

1. How did the mystery matter act as a solid? As a liquid?
2. What are some reasons why this material would act in this way?
3. What are some ways students might use this material?
4. Make a circle graph of the results.
5. Can they think of another test to try?

Suggestions for Differentiated Instruction

The students work together to try to figure out what the unknown liquids are. The teacher encourages a collaborative approach and offers suggestions of ways students can apply the knowledge of what they know about common chemicals. She suggests:

- testing different variables such as dropping a chemical on each sheet of paper to see how the papers react to the chemicals;
- shake the containers with the liquids; or
- try some possible experiments, observe, test, and be creative in your approach.

Activity 2: Demonstrating the Behavior of Molecules

Inquiry Skills: observing, comparing, hypothesizing, experimenting, and communicating.

Science Standards: inquiry, physical science, science and technology, personal perspectives, written communications.

Background Information Description

This activity simulates how molecules are connected to each other and the effect of temperature change on molecules. Students usually have questions about the way things work. The questions students naturally ask are as follows: "Why does ice cream melt?" "Why does the tea kettle burn my hand?" "Where does steam come from?" "Why is it so difficult to break rocks?"

Explain that molecules and atoms are the building blocks of matter. Heat and cold energy can change molecular form. The class is then asked to participate in the "hands-on" demonstration of how molecules work. This is a great opportunity for struggling students to participate and perhaps assume group leadership.

Before beginning the demonstration, explain that matter and energy exist and can be changed, but not created or destroyed. Ask for volunteers to role-play the parts of molecules. Direct students to join hands showing how molecules are connected to each other, explaining that this represents matter in a solid form. Next, ask them to "show what happens when a solid becomes a liquid." Heat causes the molecules to move more rapidly so that they can no longer hold themselves together. Students should drop hands and start to wiggle and move around. The next question is as follows: "How do you think molecules act when they become a gas?"

Carefully move students to the generalization that heat transforms solids into liquids and then into gases. The class enjoys watching the other students wiggle and fly around as they assumed the role of molecules turning into a gas. The last part of the demonstration is the idea that when an object is frozen, the molecules have stopped moving altogether. The demonstration and follow-up questions usually spark a lot of discussion and more questions.

Suggestions for Differentiated Instruction

Interest and student motivation are paramount in this activity. Challenge students to discover how molecules are everywhere. The students are part of a hands-on demonstration trying to answer their questions about molecules. The teacher may modify the instruction when he or she asks for volunteers to play the role of molecules even though he or she wants all students to participate. Collaborative group work is encouraged; time for discussion and lots of communication take place in this differentiated hands-on activity.

Activity 3: What Will Float?

Inquiry Skills: hypothesizing, experimenting, and communicating.

  Science Standards: inquiry, physical science, science and technology, personal perspectives, written communications.

Description
  The weight of water gives it pressure. The deeper the water, the more pressure. Pressure is also involved when something floats. For an object to float, opposing balanced forces work against each other. Gravity pulls down on the object, and the water pushes it up. The solution to floating is the object's size relevant to its weight. If it has a high volume and is light for its size, then it has a large surface area for the water to push against. In this activity, students will explore what objects will float in water. All students should try to float some of these objects.

Materials

- large plastic bowl or aquarium
- salt
- bag of small objects to test
- ruler
- paper clip, nail, block, key, etc.
- spoon
- oil-based modeling clay
- paper towels
- large washers

• kitchen foil in a 6-inch square

Procedure

1. Have the students fill the plastic bowl half full with water.
2. Direct the students to empty the bag of objects onto the table along with the other items. Next, have students separate the objects into two groups: the objects that will float and the objects that will sink. Encourage students to record their predictions in their science/math journal.
3. Have students experiment by trying to float all the objects and record what happened in their science/math journals.

Evaluation

Have students reflect on these thinking questions and respond in their science/math journals. Encourage students to work together helping students who are having trouble expressing their ideas.

1. What is alike about all the objects that floated? Sank?
2. What can be done to sink the objects that floated?
3. What can be done to float the objects that sank?
4. In what ways can a piece of foil be made to float? Sink?
5. Describe how a foil boat can be made.
6. How many washers will the foil boat carry?
7. What could float in salt water that could not float in fresh water?
8. Encourage students to try to find something that will float in fresh water and sink in salt water.

Suggestions for Differentiated Instruction

Spell out the purpose of the activity. Students have fun experimenting with what will float. Students construct boats made from aluminum foil. This motivating activity looks at water pressure, gravity, volume, weight, and ways to solve problems. The teacher differentiates by making it clear what students are to learn. She understands, appreciates, and builds on student differences, adjusting content, process, and product in response to student readiness, interests, and learning profile.

Activity 4: Exploring Water Cohesion and Surface Tension

Inquiry Skills: hypothesizing, experimenting, and communicating.

Science Standards: inquiry, earth science, science and technology, personal perspectives, written communications.

Description: Students will determine how many drops of water will fit on a penny in an experiment that demonstrates water cohesion and surface tension.

Materials

- one penny for each pair of students
- glasses of water
- paper towels
- eye droppers (one for each pair of students)

Procedures

Have students work with a partner. As a class, have them guess how many drops of water will fit on the penny. Record their guesses on the chalkboard. Ask students if it would make a difference if the penny was heads or tails. Record these guesses on the chalkboard as well. Instruct the students to try the experiment by using an eyedropper, a penny, and a glass of water.

Encourage students to record their findings in their science/math journals. Bring the class together and have each group share their findings with the whole class. Introduce the concept of cohesion. (Cohesion is the attraction of like molecules to each other. In solids and liquids, the force is strongest. It is cohesion that holds solid or liquid molecules together. There is also an attraction among water molecules for each other.) Introduce and discuss the idea of surface tension. (The molecules of water on the surface hold together so well that they often keep heavier objects from breaking through. The surface acts as if it is covered with skin.)

Evaluation, Completion, and/or Follow-Up

Have students explain how this activity showed surface tension. Instruct students to draw what surface tension looked like in their science/math journals. What makes the water drop break on the surface of the penny? (It is gravity.) What other examples can students think of in which water cohesion can be observed? (Rain on a car windshield or window in a classroom, for example.) Even disinterested students can relate to this activity if drawn into the conversation.

Suggestions for Differentiated Instruction

Teachers differentiate by modifying instruction based on their ongoing assessment of students' science knowledge. They explain what students are to learn and give them opportunities to work with a partner. Students observe, ask questions, discuss, and record their findings. Writing about surface tension is an important follow-up activity.

Activity 5: Experimenting with Surface Tension: "Soap Drops Derby"

Inquiry Skills: hypothesizing, experimenting, and communicating.

Science Standards: inquiry, physical science, science and technology, personal perspectives, written communications.

Description: Students will develop an understanding that technological solutions to problems, such as phosphate-containing detergents, have intended benefits and may have unintended consequences.

Objective: Students apply their knowledge of surface tension. This experiment shows how water acts like it has a stretchy skin because water molecules are strongly attracted to each other. Students will also be able to watch how soap molecules squeeze between the water molecules, pushing them apart and reducing the water's surface tension.

Background Information

Milk, which is mostly water, has surface tension. When the surface of milk is touched with a drop of soap, the surface tension of the milk is reduced at that spot. Since the surface tension of the milk at the soapy spot is much weaker than it is in the rest of the milk, the water molecules elsewhere in the bowl pull water molecules away from the soapy spot. The movement of the food coloring reveals these currents in the milk.

Grouping

Divide class into groups of four or five students.

Materials

- milk (only whole or 2 percent will work)
- newspapers

- a shallow container
- food coloring
- dish-washing soap
- a saucer or a plastic lid
- toothpicks

Procedures

1. Take the milk out of the refrigerator 30 minutes before the experiment starts.
2. Place the dish on the newspaper and pour about 1/2 inch of milk into the dish.
3. Let the milk sit for a minute or two.
4. Near the side of the dish, put one drop of food coloring in the milk. Place a few colored drops in a pattern around the dish. What happened?
5. Pour some dish-washing soap into the plastic lid. Dip the end of the toothpick into the soap, and touch it to the center of the milk. What happened?
6. Dip the toothpick into the soap again, and touch it to a blob of color. What happened?
7. Rub soap over the bottom half of a food-coloring bottle. Stand the bottle in the middle of the dish. What happened?

The colors can move for about 20 minutes when students keep dipping the toothpick into the soap and touching the colored drops.

Follow-Up Evaluation

Students will discuss their findings and share their outcomes with other groups. Struggling learners, along with the rest of the class, are usually excited by the "soap drops derby." Explain the history of what a "soap box derby" is (a race down a hill by kids using a wooden platform and steering apparatus). Explain to students the term "soap drops" is borrowed from the old soap box racing term. In this activity, the soap drops are racing in many directions.

NASCAR is a good example of car races. Have struggling students along with the rest of the group explain what a "soap drops derby" is and how it compares to car racing. Another question for investigation is as follows: "What unintended consequences does soap have on water molecules?"

Suggestions for Differentiated Instruction

When delivering instruction, there are many avenues for creating an instructionally responsive classroom. As you read about instructional strategies in this chapter, observe how teachers can use them to create classrooms where students have the opportunity to work at a comfortable pace, at an individually challenging degree of difficulty, and at a learning mode that is a good match for their learning profiles.

Hints for Helping All Learners

Here are a few hints that teachers can use to enhance learning for a diverse group of young people:

1. Assess students. The role of formal and informal performance assessments is to foster worthwhile learning for all students. Tools such as rubrics, checklists, and anecdotal records are some assessment strategies that are helpful for students with learning problems. Teachers may use a compacting strategy. This strategy encourages teachers to assess students before beginning a unit of study or development of a skill (Tomlinson and Cunningham Eidson, 2003).
2. Create complex instruction tasks. Complex tasks:

   • are open-ended
   • are intrinsically interesting to students
   • are uncertain (thus allowing for a variety of solutions)
   • involve real objects
   • draw upon multiple intelligences in a real-world way.

3. Use television in the classroom. Television's wide accessibility has the potential for making learning available to students who do not perform well in traditional classroom situations. It can reach students on their home ground, but the most promising place is in the classroom.
4. Use materials and activities that address a wide range of reading levels, learning profiles, and student interests. Include activities that range from simple to complex, from concrete to abstract.
5. Use science notebooks. Science notebooks are an everyday part of learning. The science notebook is more than a record of collected data

and facts of what students have learned. They are notebooks of students' questions, predictions, claims linked to evidence, conclusions, and reflections. A science notebook is a central place where language, data, and experiences work together to produce meaning for the students. Notebooks support differentiated learning. They are helpful when addressing the needs of disinterested students. In a science notebook, even students who may have poor writing skills can use visuals such as drawings, graphs, and charts to indicate their learning preferences.

There can be ongoing interaction in a notebook. For teachers, notebooks can provide a window into students' thinking and offer support for all students (Gilbert and Kotelman, 2005).

6. Provide clear directions for students. Teachers need to offer instructions about what a student can do if he or she needs help.

7. Use a record-keeping system to monitor what students do.

8. Include a plan for ongoing assessment. Teachers use ongoing assessments of student readiness, interest, and learning profile for the purpose of matching tasks to students' needs. Some students struggle with many things, while others are more advanced, but most have areas of weakness. So it is best not to assume that one set of skills can be mastered in the same way by everybody.

For the teacher: Meeting the needs of all students requires finding relationships among science, math, technology, and students' life experiences. Being able to deal with criticism and mistakes is crucial to creative scientific behavior. Some scientists use failure as manure for the next experiment.

If you're not prepared to be wrong, you'll never come up with anything original.

—Ken Robinson

Preparing Scientifically Literate Citizens

One of the important new goals of American education is to prepare scientifically literate citizens. This means preparing students who can make use of scientific knowledge and connect the implications of science to their personal lives and to society. Scientific literacy also involves having a broad familiarity with today's scientific issues and the key concepts that underlie them.

As far as the schools are concerned, scientific literacy has a lot to do with organizing scientific inquiry around real-life inquiry and creative problem solving. A good problem or question can usually elicit critical thinking and shared decision making. Curiosity, observation, posing questions, and actively seeking answers are all part of the process (Honey and Kanter, 2013).

The recognized importance of a scientifically literate citizenry has had a lot to do with developing standards for science education. Seasoned teachers know that effective teaching strategies should include concrete, physical experiences and opportunities for students to explore science in their lives.

Active science learning connects students with the past, the present, and the science-influenced world of tomorrow. Teachers are increasingly connecting learning about science to responsible citizenship and self-understanding. Goals include using scientific knowledge in making wise decisions and solving difficult problems related to life and living.

Science instruction today places an increased emphasis on encouraging students to connect science learning with the development of critical thinking and imaginative problem-solving skills. It also makes sense to actively involve students in the learning process in ways that stimulate the development of effective oral and written communication skills.

In the modern science classroom, collaborative group activity is common; students are provided with many opportunities to question data and to design and conduct real experiments. In addition, learners are encouraged to carry their thinking beyond the class experience.

It is important for students to raise questions that are appealing and familiar to them. Such activities can improve reasoning and collaborative decision making. This is especially true when learning is done in small cohesive groups that share ideas and strengths (Sherman et al., 2005).

Science can be an exciting experience for students and teachers when it is taught as an active hands-on subject. Connecting with other disciplines can provide many opportunities for integration with other subjects. Asking an elementary-school teacher to be an expert in the dozens of subjects he/she has to teach is unreasonable.

If there are many cultures and home languages in the classroom, the teacher will have to make an effort to gain insights into the cultural experiences of others. And he/she will have to figure out the best way to encourage an increasingly diverse student body.

All teachers need at least some depth of knowledge in the subjects that they are teaching. And their content knowledge needs to be broad enough to work with second-language learners and others who may have difficulty with their schoolwork. With students whose first language is not English, educators may have to spend some time improving language and developing literacy along the road to content mastery.

Understanding and using science today require an awareness of how science connects language and technology domains—as well as how science relates to our culture and our lives. As far as teaching is concerned, it is important to build up a science knowledge base and develop a repertoire of current pedagogical techniques.

By focusing on real investigations and active learning, teachers can move students from the concrete to the abstract by exploring broad themes that connect multiple subjects. Modern learning strategies include many participatory experiences—as well as many opportunities for students to explore the influence of science in their lives.

Active Learning, Scientific Inquiry, and Inclusion

As a field of study, science is becoming increasingly interdisciplinary. For example, some of the new research fields emerging include biochemistry, biophysics, plant engineering, terrestrial biology, and neurobiology, to name a few. Some of these changes are reflected in the standards and in the textbooks; some are not.

Students can develop effective interpersonal skills as they work together, pose questions, and critically examine data. This often means designing and conducting real-world experiments that carry their thinking beyond the classroom. As instruction becomes more connected to students' lives, enriching possibilities arise from inquiring about real-world concerns.

We should all strive to make sure that play, passion, and purpose are part of every child's framework for scientific reasoning and experimentation. Scientific inquiry also involves posing questions, making observations, conducting investigations, providing explanations, and communicating the results.

All young people should have the chance to learn and actually do science as they travel down the road to scientific literacy. This was one of the themes in *The Next Generation Science Standards* (2013). The standards also emphasize the processes of science and give a great deal of attention to cognitive abilities such as logic, evidence, and extending knowledge to construct explanations of natural phenomena.

Scientific literacy should begin in the early grades, when students are naturally curious and eager to explore. Another theme in the standards is that science is an active process. Getting students actively involved in the process or the *doing* of science moves students along the road to scientific awareness.

Learning the fundamentally important facts, concepts, and skills of science certainly matters. But just as fundamental is the disciplined use of knowledge: inquiry and problem solving. Concepts and inquiry are both fundamental skills that students must begin developing early on.

Outside of school, scientific truth is elusive in a culture that is being swamped with stuff that looks like information but is often something a little more suspicious. Being able use the scientific method (processes) to sort things out would certainly help. Also, skeptical inquiry skills are needed to sort through the multimedia collage of material that passes by students in the blink of an eye.

At school, the basics of science and scientific reasoning must go hand in hand if we are going to motivate all students to learn science. The first thing for teachers is figuring out their students' current understanding of scientific ideas. The next step is moving away from everyday ways of talking about natural phenomena toward more scientific ways of examining and discussing subjects.

Being aware of the scientific method and creative problem solving is now a necessary skill for everyone. With the help of investigative experiences and collaborative inquiry, even the more reluctant learners can be motivated to learn how to apply scientific processes and recognize where their thinking is breaking down.

The old approach of feeding struggling students a diet based on the old chalk, talk, and memorize routine will not go a long way toward engaging today's students.

As any teacher will tell you, reluctant learners can be a challenge, especially when it comes to science and math. But there are powerful opportunities—especially when teachers add some joy, excitement, and interaction to the learning process.

SUMMARY, CONCLUSION, AND LOOKING AHEAD

Science education today is strongly influenced by the national standards, professional associations, school textbooks, and state requirements. In spite of the different voices involved, there is general agreement that a key science-teaching goal should be creating a climate of possibility for all students.

In the United States, state agencies generally have more influence than anyone at the federal level. School districts are major players because much of what takes place in school is under local control. But in the classroom, teachers are the key decision makers when it comes to how something gets taught.

Everyone involved in education decision making could use a better vocabulary to address the future of science education. But in the meantime, it is important to recognize that total agreement may not always be possible and major players have to collaborate if science instruction is going to shine.

Increasingly, educators approach science instruction in a way that builds on mixed-ability groups, different cultures, and paying close attention to second-language learners. In such a setting, teachers differentiate by providing different routes to content, activities, and products in order to meet an increasingly diverse set of student needs. A one-size-fits-all delivery system simply will not get the job done.

In today's social and educational environment, it is no longer enough to provide some students with a quality science curriculum (in preparation for college) and others with the bare outlines of scientific facts. Now there is general recognition that every student must be involved in inquiry-based science instruction in order to succeed in the workplace and act as an informed citizen (Gorman et al., 2013).

It is important to involve all learners in a process of asking questions, exploring, and making connections that lead to discovery—whether they are struggling students or advanced learners. The basic idea is to make sure that all learners acquire the appropriate level of scientific knowledge and science understanding.

Regardless of whether a student initially likes science, it makes sense to set up intellectual challenges that build on individual interests and abilities. It is also important to structure lessons in a way that moves everyone in the classroom in the direction of developing and sustaining a high level of curiosity and engagement.

Educators have long recognized that science education should not be isolated from day-to-day realities and technological progress. At every grade level, science education has dimensions that extend to the social sciences as well as ethics, values, and communication technologies. An essential question is how science instruction can create the next generation of innovators and affect the direction of change.

If you're looking for new answers, think of new questions.

—Anonymous

Science education today strives to reflect human values and help students move in the direction of taking responsibility for the natural world. In the wired world of the twenty-first century, it is important for students to realize that we are all part of a global community. And it is a community in which the sciences are transforming the relationship between human beings and the earth's ecosystems.

The advance of global connectivity is bound to impact both the physical and the virtual worlds. In such an environment, an important skill involves learning how to navigate an increasingly multidimensional world that has an electronic nervous system.

Forces that drive young innovators include knowing the art of traveling rivers of information, crossing divides, and pushing boundaries. The students in school today are going to be spending a lot of time wrestling with unprecedented challenges in the future, so they had better get ready to deal with innovation-driven change today.

Science distinguishes itself from other ways of knowing and from other bodies of knowledge through the use of empirical standards, collaborative inquiry, logical arguments, and skepticism.

—National Research Council

QUESTIONS FOR TEACHERS AND PROSPECTIVE TEACHERS

1. Why are some students reluctant to participate in science lessons? What can you do to make science more attractive for all learners?
2. How might you design a science lesson that allows for differences in students' prior knowledge, learning styles, interests, and socialization needs?
3. What is your personal image of science and scientists? Draw a picture of a scientist. Share with peers.
4. Think of a science question you are curious about. How might it generate scientific interest in others?

5. Get together with someone else and compare questions. See if the two of you come up with a good question. Form a hypothesis.
6. Do some research or perform an experiment that proves or disproves your hypothesis. Present your findings to your professional peers.

REFERENCES AND RESOURCES

Benjamin, A. (2003). *Differentiated Instruction: A Guide for Elementary School Teachers.* Larchmont, NY: Eye On Education.

Dixon-Krauss, L. (1996). *Vygotsky in the Classroom.* Upper Saddle River, NJ: Pearson Education.

Gilbert, J., & Kotelman, M. (2005). "Five Good Reasons to Use Science Notebooks." *Science & Children* 43 (3): 28–32.

Gorman, M., Tweney, R., Gooding, D., & Kincannon, A., eds. (2013). *Scientific and Technical Thinking.* New York, NY: Routledge.

Honey, M., & Kanter, D. (2013). *Growing the Text Generation of STEM Innovators.* New York, NY: Routledge.

de Mauro, L. (2005). *Thomas Edison: A Brilliant Inventor.* New York, NY: HarperCollins [TIME for Kids].

Morozov, E. (2013). *To Save Everything, Click Here: The Folly of Technological Solutionism.* New York, NY: PublicAffairs, A Perseus Books Group.

National Academies Press (1996). *National Science Education Standards.* Washington, DC: National Academy Press.

National Research Council (NRC). (2000). *Inquiry and the National Science Education Standards.* Washington, DC: National Academy Press.

National Research Council (NRC). (2012). *A Framework for K–12 Science Education: Practices, Crosscutting Concepts, and Core Ideas.* Washington, DC: National Academies Press.

NGSS Lead States (2013). *The Next Generation Science Standards.* Washington, DC: National Academies Press.

Robinson, K. (2013). *Finding Your Element: How to Discover Your Talents and Passions and Transform Your Life.* New York, NY: Viking.

Sherman, H., Richardson, L., & Yard, G. (2005). *Teaching Children Who Struggle with Mathematics: A Systematic Approach to Analysis and Correction.* Upper Saddle River, NJ: Prentice Hall/Pearson.

Smolin, L. (2013). *Time Reborn: From the Crisis in Physics to the Future of the Universe.* New York, NY: Houghton Mifflin Harcourt.

Tomlinson, C., & Cunningham Eidson, C. (2003). *Differentiation in Practice: A Resource Guide for Differentiating Curriculum.* Alexandria, VA: Association for Supervision and Curriculum Development.

Wickman, P. (2013). *Aesthetic Experience in Science Education.* New York, NY: Routledge.

Chapter Five

Technology: The Powerful Possibilities of Tools

It is through the beauty of personal and group discovery that one proceeds to self-reliant learning, deep knowledge, and freedom.

—Friedrich Schiller

In this chapter, you will find ideas, practical suggestions, and lesson plans that are designed to help students gain an understanding of the technological products of math and science. The goal is to help assist educators as they try to help students use and more deeply understand the impact of digital technology.

A little healthy skepticism about the benefits of technology has to be part of the discussion. This means giving attention to the myths, as well as the magic.

If there ever was a dividing line between cyberspace and "the real world," it is rapidly vanishing. In such an environment, some understanding of the effect of Internet access to the world of ideas is part of what it takes now to be both personally and academically engaged.

Computers, big data, and their digital associates are useful in searching for needles in a haystack. But how useful are they in improving the dimensions of skills that matter most in the innovation-driven world of today?

Knowing how to evaluate the glut of information available across the full spectrum of media and devices is now part of what it means to be literate. For example, online there are few comments that can be fully trusted when it comes to the millions of online voices and the masks out there.

Can you sort out either the good people or the good information from the bad? On the Internet, you do not know who is who or what is what—and yes, you should care.

To some extent, all of the content standards suggest that it is important to recognize and examine the promises, pitfalls, and social effects of converging technologies. The standards in math, science, and technology can assist teachers as they work to teach content in a way that helps young people navigate through a rapidly changing technological world.

The technological products of science and math are an increasingly powerful force for social development, learning, and innovation. In the classroom, the ability to use technology to solve problems creatively can help students bring imaginative possibilities to life. So it is little wonder that understanding the implications of a world filled with the technological by-products of mathematics and science is viewed as a necessity for everyone (Morozov, 2012).

At school, teachers are striving to make subject matter fresh and help students develop unique perspectives for edging into the future. Recent advances in microelectronics, nanotechnology, information theory, and synthetic biology are but a few of the new possibilities for imaginative study. Still, many have found that is easier to teach students how to use the latest high-tech devices and apps than it is to help learners develop more important skills like creative reasoning, critical thinking, and collaboration.

All of us seem to be spending more and more time with digital technology. Now there are even thousands of apps specifically designed for preschool children. And there is much more is out there for school-age youngsters. But too few questions have been asked about how computers, tablets, smartphones, and other whiz-bang gadgets affect learning and youngsters' brains.

Opening doors to math, science, and technology has a lot to do with helping young people develop the skills to eventually influence the direction of technological change and help them be more comfortable with innovation. Lifelong learning, constant personal change, and handling the impact of unpredictable events are just a few of the essential facts of life in the twenty-first century (Lanier, 2013).

In any future, we must all constantly invent and reinvent personal and professional methodologies. New technological tools open up infinite possibilities. Just keep in mind the fact that new channels for information and communication are being built on an understanding of basic subjects, reasoning, and collaboration.

LEARNING AT ITS BEST IS A SOCIAL ACTIVITY

Learning and creativity often happen in conversation with others. Technology can get in the way or it can help create the next generation of innovators. What is most important is to make sure that people are in control—rather than the other way around.

"Present shock," in which everything happens right now, is yet another problem the touch-screen generation has to learn how to tame. Just one example: What you post today may be around forever. Of course, there are always issues with technology—you just have to learn how to deal with them.

Technological tools of one kind or another have long been an intrinsic part of all cultural and educational systems. But digital technologies have amplified a world changing at an increasingly dizzying tempo. When using such technology in school, it is important that all students go beyond worksheet-type, on-screen experiences.

Quality instruction involves engaging students in higher-level thinking, collaborative inquiry, problem solving, and meaningful communication. Educating thoughtful young people also relies on teachers who can help students develop the skills and motivation required to advance academic competence. In addition, what students can actually *do* with what they learn and understand increases their potential for contributing to the well-being of the community.

Educators realize that they must help their students ask essential questions and take advantage of the fact that current technology could help them come up with informed answers (McTighe and Wiggens, 2013). Digital devices, apps, and the Internet are important things, but they are far from being the only things.

Collaborative work and low-tech possibilities have major roles to play in the classroom. Simple math and science manipulatives, for example, are very useful on their own. And they can go hand in hand with incorporating digital technology and the Internet into daily lessons.

The increasingly complex problems facing humanity and students are largely caused by human and natural factors. Technology can help or it can be a distraction in a future that is bound *not* be what it used to be. But whatever is out there, just beyond the horizon, will favor young people who understand technology, face up to unexpected challenges, and are well educated.

However teachers go about preparing youngsters for the unpredictable, as soon as this Monday, they have to continue to do their best to reach and motivate all students in their classroom. To accomplish this task, they have to use all the tools available to meet different student needs and interests.

Considering Student Differences

Students need to approach science, math, and technology in different ways to more fully understand these subjects. The term *differentiated instruction* is often applied to a variety of classroom practices that allow for the differences in student interests, prior knowledge, socialization needs, and learning styles. It can also be used to describe the degree of individual structure in a lesson, pacing, complexity, and level of abstraction.

Differentiation in content area work has proven to be an effective way to reach all students. The basic idea is that learning happens when adjustments are made so that a learner at any achievement level can make sense (meaning) out of the information and concepts being taught (Benjamin, 2005).

Although electronic technology is the emphasis here, the standards make it clear that both high-tech (computers) and low-tech (simple manipulatives) are essential to inquiry in science and problem solving in mathematics. The standards also suggest ways of improving science and math instruction for all students, including those who are having difficulty with these subjects.

Clearly, all students should have access to the same high-quality content to ensure that they meet similar learning goals. The underlying assumption is that underachieving students should not be limited to executing math rules and remembering only basic science concepts. Aiming low just does not get the job done. When in doubt, it is best to "teach up" with strategies that engage the imagination with the help of active learning and group participation.

From inquiry into natural world (science) processes to problem solving in mathematics, technological designs and tools have constraints that limit our choices. Part of the excitement has always been not knowing when the boundaries of effectiveness will shift and where things will end up. One example of a surprise that awaits us is associated with learning about the architecture of information storage in the mind.

Where math, science, and their technological associates are taking us remains something of a mystery. Some of the consequences can be predicted. Many cannot. For example, who at the beginning of the twentieth century would have predicted the human consequences of physics and the technologies associated with atomic energy?

Technology shapes *and* reflects the values found in society. At school, it can isolate learners *or* help them join with others. In our personal and civic lives, technological tools frequently slip through our hands to limit our choices at work and erode the edges of the constitutional rights of privacy in our daily lives (Thompson, 2013).

On one level, digital technology and globalization empower individuals and diminish governments. On another, it can bring out the worst in human nature and diminish the imagination. Those who think that it is all good or all bad just do not get it. Heaven help those who do not want to get caught up in dealing with a glut of information.

In spite of some nuisances and misplaced enthusiasm, computer-based technology is now an essential part of math and science instruction. At its out-of-school worst, it is frequently associated with rigidly preprogrammed arcade-like shoot 'em ups in which children frantically click on icons for instant gratification. At school, computers and the Internet can turn mathematics and science into spectator sports. As usual, digital technology is a double-edged sword.

Digital technologies can be excellent vehicles for questioning, investigating, analyzing, simulating, and communicating. At their best, technological tools allow you to take control, solve problems, inquire collaboratively, and observe phenomena that would otherwise remain unobservable.

THE STANDARDS AND CONNECTING WITH STUDENTS

The science, math, and technology standards view technology as a means to form connections between the natural and manmade worlds. There is general agreement that it is important to pay attention to technological design and how technology can help students understand the big ideas of mathematics and science. The standards also suggest that all students at every grade level be given opportunities to use all kinds of low-tech and high-tech technologies to explore and design solutions to problems.

For example, find themes that help students see the human factor and its societal implications. The laws of the physical and biological universe are viewed as important to understanding how technological objects and systems work. The standards also point to the importance of connecting students to the various elements of our technologically intensive world so that they can construct models and solve problems with technology.

NATIONAL EDUCATIONAL TECHNOLOGY STANDARDS

The International Society for Technology in Education (ISTE) has developed a set of performance indicators and guidelines for technology-literate students and teachers. Their technology foundation standards for students are divided into six categories and provide guidelines for structuring related activities.

1. Basic operations and concepts

    *   Students demonstrate knowledge of the nature and operation of technology systems.
    *   Students are proficient in the use of technology.

2. Social, ethical, and human issues

    *   Students understand the ethical, cultural, and societal issues related to technology.
    *   Students practice responsible use of technology systems, information, and software.
    *   Students develop positive attitudes toward technology uses that support lifelong learning, collaboration, personal pursuits, and productivity.

3. Technology productivity tools

    *   Students use technology tools to enhance learning, increase productivity, and promote creativity.
    *   Students use productivity tools to collaborate in constructing technology-enhanced models, prepare publications, and promote other creative works.

4. Technology communication tools

    *   Students use telecommunications to collaborate, publish, and interact with peers, experts, and other audiences.

- Students use a variety of media and formats to communicate information and ideas effectively to multiple audiences.

5. Technology research tools

- Students use technology to locate, evaluate, and collect information from a variety of sources.
- Students use technology tools to process data and report results.
- Students evaluate and select new information resources and technological innovations based on the appropriateness for specific tasks.

6. Technology problem-solving and decision-making tools

- Students use technology resources for solving problems and making informed decisions.
- Students employ technology for solving problems in the real world. (International Educational Technology Association, 2000)

Through the ongoing use of technology in the schooling process, students are empowered to achieve important technology capabilities. The key individual in helping students develop those capabilities is the classroom teacher.
—International Society for Technology in Education (ISTE)
NETS*T project, 2000

Technology Samples from the Mathematics Standards

The National Council of Teachers of Mathematics (NCTM) Standards include the use of technology in their core beliefs about students, teaching, learning, and mathematics. Many situations that arise in the classroom afford opportunities for the application of mathematical skills and the use of technological tools like calculators.

Calculators are recommended for school mathematics programs to help students develop number sense, problem-solving skills, mental computation, and estimation. They also help develop the ability to see patterns, perform operations, and use graphics.

Calculators and other forms of technology continue to be used extensively in the home and office. The cost of calculators and other forms of technology continues to decrease, while their power and functions continue to increase. Curriculum documents increasingly encourage the use of calculators and other forms of technology. Some tests currently available allow and even encourage calculator use (Cathcart et al., 2010).

Exploring Math Activities with High- and Low-Tech Tools

Start by asking students to bring something to school that goes back into technological history. It could be from last week or many decades ago. Everything from paper and pencil to old calculators and the latest mobile gadgets. (Just ask them to make sure that what they bring in still works.)

Divide students into groups of two or three and have them explore the history of the objects and experiment with the devices in their group. Create a timeline for their devices and try some math problems with each one.

The new mathematics recommendations specify that digital devices should be made available some of the time, especially for doing homework, class assignments, and tests. The following activities are just some suggestions for how you might use digital devices in your class.

1. Improving Addition and Subtraction Estimation Skills

Select two teams of students. Provide a calculator for each student. As play begins, one member from the first team says a three-digit number. A player from the second team says another three-digit number. Both players silently write an estimate of the sum of the two numbers. Players are limited to a five-second time limit to make estimates. Then both players use the device to determine the sum. The player whose estimate is closest to the actual sum scores a point for the team. In case of a tie, both teams earn a point. The next player on each team assumes the same role.

The rules for subtraction are similar. One player from each team names a three-digit number. Both players then write down their estimates of the difference between the two numbers. Again, the player whose estimate is closest to the actual difference earns a point for the team. Students who engage in this activity for a while develop estimation strategies that benefit them in and out of the classroom.

2. Multiplication Puzzlers

For each problem, find the missing number by using the calculator and the problem-solving strategy of guessing and checking. Do not solve the problems by dividing; instead, see how many guesses each takes you. Record all of your guesses. For example, 4 × ___ = 87. You might start with 23 and then adjust. Below is a possible solution that shows you how to record.

4 × 23 = 92
4 × 22 = 88
4 × 21 = 84
4 × 21.5 = 86
4 × 21.6 = 86.4
4 × 21.7 = 86.8
4 × 21.8 = 87.2
4 × 21.74 = 86.96
4 × 21.75 = 87

3. Solve Problems [How Many Seconds Old Are You?]

Students may need to become familiar with the directions—how many seconds in a minute, a day, a month, a year? It is good to define the parameters. How old will you be at noon today? Encourage students to take a guess. Have them write it down. Use a calculator to find out. The problem requires several phases to its solution:

a. Decide what information is needed and where to collect it.
b. Choose the numerical information to use.
c. Do the necessary calculations.
d. Use judgment to interpret the results and make decisions about a possible solution.

4. Skip Counting

Try skip counting. Encourage students to count by 100s and 1,000s. Or try skip counting by 3s, 5s, 7s, 9s, or whatever. You can begin counting with any number and skip count by any number. Have students try these calculator counting exercises, then have them make up their own. Encourage speculation about what the next number will be. Can you find a pattern?

Try having a counting race. How long does it take counting by 1s to count to 1,000? How long would it take counting by hundreds to count to 1,000,000?

Technology Samples from the Science Standards

Students Should Have an Understanding of Science and Technology

The science and technology standards connect students to the designed world and introduce them to the laws of nature through their understandings of how technological objects and systems work. People have always invented tools to help find answers to the many questions they have about their world. Just as scientists and engineers work in teams to get results, so should students work in teams that combine scientist and engineering talents (Wenglinsky, 2005).

Developing Technological Design Ability

This standard begins the understanding of the design process, as well as the solving of simple design problems. Children's abilities in technological problem solving can be developed by firsthand experience by studying technological products and systems in their world.

We agree with the idea that the problem-solving ability of children can be developed by firsthand experiences in which they use technological tools similar to those used by mathematicians, scientists, and engineers. Of course, computers and the Internet are important. But, as the standards point out, students should also see the technological products and systems found in the relatively low-tech world of zippers, can openers, and math manipulatives.

With or without digital technology, even young children can engage in projects that are appropriately challenging for them—ones in which they may design ways to fasten, ways to move, or ways to communicate more effectively.

Students begin to understand the design process as well as improve their ability to solve simple problems. Even when solving simple problems in which they are trying to meet certain criteria, students will find elements of math, science, and technology that can be powerful aids.

At higher grade levels, lessons can include examples of technological achievements in which math and science have played a part. Students can also be encouraged to examine where technical advances have contributed directly to scientific progress. To consider the other side of the coin, they can look at occasions when the products of science and math have hurt the environment and taken away jobs.

Students of all ages should have many experiences that involve math, science, math, and technological applications (Bers, 2007). Some of these are as simple as measuring and weighing various objects on a balance scale. These activities can teach math and science skills such as comparing, estimating, predicting, and recording data. What is the technology connection?

A scale is one of the relatively simple technological tools used in mathematics and science for measuring mass or weight. Too frequently, however, teachers forget to mention the technological connection. Whether it is simple or complex, bathroom scales or hot new computers, the technology in our day-to-day world is often misunderstood—and it is difficult to escape.

All students can be motivated by studying existing products: their functions, the problems they solve, the materials used in their construction, and how well they do what they are supposed to do. A common technological device, like a vegetable or cheese grater, can be used as an object for students to investigate. Have students figure out what it does, how it helps people, and what problems it might solve and cause. Such student problems provide excellent opportunities to direct attention to a specific technology—the tools and instruments used in mathematics and science.

In the early elementary grades, many of the tasks can be designed around the familiar contexts of the home, school, and community. Also, at early levels, problems should be clear and have only one or two solutions that do not require a great deal of preparation time or complicated assembly. As the standards in math and science make clear, students can learn a great deal about both subjects from the low-tech *and* the high-tech ends of the technology spectrum.

As we consider extending preschool education, it is important to recognize the fact that a child's early literacy environment goes a long way toward determining future school success. Middle-class children hear far more words than poor children—and it makes a big difference.

Many curriculum programs and some state guidelines suggest that teachers at all levels should integrate math, science, technology, and communication skills with social issues. This means encouraging a multidisciplinary analysis of problems that are relevant to their world.

A sequence of five stages is usually involved in the technology-based problem-solving process: (1) identifying and stating the problem, (2) designing an approach to solving the problem, (3) implementing and arriving at a solution, (4) evaluating results, and (5) communicating the problem, design, and solution. In keeping with the standards document, teachers may also have elementary and middle-school students design problems and technological investigations which incorporate several interesting issues in math and science.

By using a variety of materials and technologies for mathematical problem solving and scientific inquiry, students may recognize (as many have suggested) that education is more than preparing for life—it is life itself.

Emerging Technologies in the Science Classroom

Emerging technologies are technologies that are just getting started in K–12 classrooms and are being explored as new tools to help students gain a better understanding of science and improve student achievement. With the recent improvements in wireless technologies, small mobile computers, iPods, and Internet-connecting cellphones, schools are examining the use of personal digital assistants in their classrooms. Sometimes they are disruptive, and sometimes they are helpful. Local districts and teachers have to set the limits. However, the use of digital technological tools such as the graphing calculator, motion detectors, and various scientific instruments has a proven track record.

Graphing calculators and Calculator-Based Laboratory (CBL) probes capture real data and generate a scatter plot of data. Good exploratory questions can be asked to generate more interesting functional relationships. For example, ask students to create a linear descending line, an increasing line, a parabola, a horizontal line, and a vertical line using a motion detector. They will find this challenging, perhaps even impossible. Using probes and calculators allows students to look for patterns and to generalize many realistic formulas resulting from the graph of the data. The graphing calculator's statistical options allow for a formula or function relationship to emerge (Cathcart et al., 2010).

Just as the National Science Education Standards suggest how a science concept can be learned, the International Society for Technology in Education recommends that the teaching of the International Technology Standards should not take place void of content.

The lessons that follow here can be accomplished without the use of educational technology. However, as you read through the technology standards, you will discover that by applying a few of these suggestions to the lessons, educational technology can enrich the learning experience.

ACTIVITIES TO MOTIVATE ALL LEARNERS

Activity Title: The Egg-Catching Contest

Inquiry Question: Can you design a container that can keep a raw egg from breaking when dropped from the ceiling?

Concept: Students will design and test a container that can protect a raw egg.

Purpose and Objectives: This is an example of a design activity that meets the math/science/technology standards. Students will design and test a container that can keep a raw egg from breaking when dropped from five, six, or seven feet in the air.

Materials

- Soft packing materials such as styrofoam peanuts, cotton, paper towels, bubble wrap
- Creative devices such as pudding, water, containers, pillow, etc.
- Materials from home to finish the group's design

Procedures

This technology activity should be preceded by a math and science unit on force and motion so that students are able to apply their knowledge of mathematics and science in their design process. Divide the class into groups of about four students each. Explain that each group is responsible for planning the egg-catching design. Emphasize creativity. The egg catcher must be 12 inches off the floor.

Explain the problem or challenge. Your group must work together to:

- brainstorm ideas
- sketch a design
- formulate a rationale
- assign group tasks—including clean-up crew
- get materials
- build the container
- try several tests
- perform a class demonstration

Evaluation, Completion and/or Follow-Up

The presentation will begin with a discussion of what their group has done to meet the challenge. Assessment for the egg catcher is not whether the egg broke, but rather how they were able to share what they found out as they tried to solve the problem and prepared for a successful attempt. It is helpful to have the class make a video of the presentation. It can be viewed again by the designers and by parents, or it can be used in other class sessions in years to come.

Activity Title: Design and Build a City

Inquiry Question: How are cities planned?

Concept: Among other things, city planning involves examining maps, collecting data, designing, and planning for construction.

Purpose and Objectives: This is an example of a design activity that meets the math/science/technology standards.

Another interesting problem for middle-school students is to design and build a city. Students are instructed to design a city with an efficient road network. They must also create an election process that ensures that the city council fairly represents all city residents. In addition, students must contact construction companies and make a plan for building their cities.

To prepare for this challenge, students have to learn about routing graphs, which are used to plan routes for mail carriers and garbage carriers so they do not waste steps or gas unnecessarily. Contractors also use routing graphs to plan roads in new residential communities. Students collaborate in groups, analyzing their decisions by writing a rationale for their design decisions. They must also make a fifteen-minute oral presentation to "sell" their cities. This project allows students to be creative in applying the science, math, and technology applications they have learned. Some students have created their cities on islands, on the moon—even underground.

Activity Title: Other Bright Science and Math Ideas

Inquiry Question: What kind of devices can you create to make your life easier?

Concept: Creative ideas can be developed by everyone.

Purpose and Objectives: This is an example of a design activity that meets the math/science/technology standards. Innovative ideas can be low tech. Some low-tech activities might include the following: (1) designing a device to keep pencils from rolling off your desk; (2) creating something that is easy to make that tastes good and would fit in your lunch box; (3) designing a device that would shield your eyes from the sun; (4) creating an instrument that would make lifting easier; and (5) designing ways to save money on school supplies.

ACTIVITIES FOR UNDERSTANDING COMMUNICATIONS TECHNOLOGY

Activity Title: Communications Timeline

Inquiry Question: How have communications changed over time?

Concept: History influences how people communicate. The ways in which people communicate with each other have changed throughout history. In ancient days, cave painting conveyed messages and created meaning for people. For centuries, storytelling and oral language served as the primary means of communicating information. Handwritten manuscripts were the first written for communication, followed more recently by the printing press, telegraph, typewriter, telephone, radio, television, computers, and video cellphone. The list could go on.

Purpose and Objectives: This is an example of a design activity that meets the math/science/technology standards.

Through this activity, students will research the history of communications technology and create a timeline in their math/science journal. This activity allows students to collect as many actual objects as possible or their representations for display. They will explain in writing how these communications devices work, talk about and share ideas with others, and answer any questions the class raises.

Materials: reference books, science/math journals, communication devices from home, grandparents, community, or elsewhere.

Procedure

1. Have students research the history of communications technology and create a timeline. Have them put their notes in their math/science journal.
2. Encourage students to assemble a communications timeline project for display, using as many actual objects or their representations as possible.

3. Remind students that each time period needs to have some examples of the actual objects used and a written explanation about these communications devices.

Evaluation/Extension

1. Direct students to choose a communications technique from the past. Teachers may wish to divide students into groups according to interests and assign each group a certain time period or technological tool used for communication.
2. Direct groups to orally (and perhaps graphically) present their communication tool to the class.
3. Teachers may extend the project by having students project what communications of the future will look like.

Activity Title: Create a Water Clock

Inquiry Question: How do clocks work?

Concept: Clocks keep track of time. (Time is frequently a difficult concept for children to grasp. People have recorded the passage of time throughout history.)

Purpose and Objectives: This is an example of a design activity that meets the math/science/technology standards.

This activity involves children involved in time measurement by using a number of old and new technological tools. Students will learn how to measure time using a variety of clocks.

Materials

- a variety of large cans, plastic bottles, and plastic containers
- a collection of corks or plugs
- modeling clay
- scissors or knife
- hammer and nail with large head
- math and science journal

Procedures

Have students collect a variety of large cans, plastic bottles, and plastic containers. You may wish to help them make a small hole in the bottom of the metal containers either with a hammer and a large nail or with plastic containers using a scissors or a knife (try to make all of the holes in the containers the same size). Instruct students to make a clay plug or a small cork to fit the hole. Have students fill the containers with water, then release the plugs and compare the times of each container. Encourage students to guess which one will empty first.

Evaluation/Follow-Up

1. Have students choose common jobs that can be timed with water clocks.
2. Encourage students to make a list of things that can be timed with a water clock.
3. Instruct students to hypothesize on the effects of different-sized holes on the water drip process.
4. Have students use a digital clock to determine how much water flows out in one minute's time from their water clock.
5. Ask students to design a system to mark their water clock to determine the time without measuring the water level each time.
6. Ask students if they can make a clock another way.
7. Have students write a program for a computer to record time.

Follow-Up Questions

Instruct students to respond to these questions in their math/science journal:

• Why are clocks so important to the industrial age?
• How are clocks used as metaphors?
• Encourage students to speculate on the future of clocks and their role in the future.

Activity Title: Hypothesis Testing

Inquiry Question: How do I find out?

Concept: This technology awareness activity is designed to get students involved in the historic role of technology in today's society.

Purpose and Objectives: Students will conduct inquiry in trying to discover what technological devices are being presented. Students will reinforce their skills of questioning, observing, communicating, and making inferences. This is an example of a design activity that meets the math/science/technology standards.

Materials: Instruct students to bring in a paper bag with the following contents:

- one item that no one would be able to recognize (an old tool of their grandfather's, for example)
- one item that some people may be able to identify
- one common item that everyone would recognize

Procedure

1. Divide students into small groups. Tell students that all items in their bags should be kept secret.
2. Give the students the following directions:

   a. There will be no talking in the first part of this activity.
   b. Each student will exchange bags with someone else in the group.
   c. Students may then open their bags, remove one item, and write down what they think that item is. Have students examine each item carefully. Also have students write their reaction to how they feel about this item, what they think it may be used for, and which category this item falls into (common item, one no one would recognize, etc.).

3. Repeat with each of the items in the bag.
4. Students will then exchange bags with those of other groups and go through the same procedure.

Evaluation, Completion, and Follow-Up
When everyone has finished examining their bag of articles and written their responses, they will meet back together in their group and explain what they have discovered in their bags. Encourage class speculation, questions, and guesses about unidentified items. The student who brought the unknown tool or article in should be responsible for answering the questions posed, but the identity must not be given away until all guesses and hypotheses have been raised.

ASKING COMMUNICATION QUESTIONS

An example: How could an Internet breakdown harm the whole world, a country, a city, or an individual?

A Little Background Information

The Internet is now wired into everything from airline fleets to power grids to Web-enabled security systems for home and office. Cloud computing adds to the vulnerability, as it involves the use of server farms, all over the world, where companies and people outsource hardware and software. Clients, whether they are individuals or organizations, rent, lease, or pay for the use of information technology resources of third-party service providers (in this case, the cloud service providers) to gain access to software, hardware assets, information technology platform services, and so forth.

Cloud computing services are nothing new—most people who use free e-mail services rely on the cloud for the storage of their e-mail messages. The obvious upside here is that customers can save a lot money that they would otherwise have to spend if they purchased and owned their information technology assets. Nowadays, it makes little sense to own information technology because of the very fast rate of change leading to rapid technology obsolescence.

Major organizations like the New York Stock Exchange and Dow Chemical Company use cloud computing services. Even big governmental agencies are now relying heavily on vulnerable cloud computing. (The CIA has hired Amazon to build a private cloud that has more security features.)

Reliance on the Internet in daily life has grown before anyone has come to terms with the risks involved. It goes well beyond being a digital challenge; it is a physical problem as well.

What are the possible side effects of a catastrophic event in cyberspace?

Experienced teachers know what works best when it comes engaging and exciting students.

How Does Technology Change Things in the Classroom?

Digital technology changes math and science instruction by changing the classroom environment and providing opportunities for students to create new knowledge for themselves. It goes beyond the "telling" model of instruction that many underachieving students find so problematic. Instead, technology can be used in many ways to encourage students to learn by doing.

Various digital technologies and related applications can serve as vehicles for discovery-based classrooms—giving students access to data, experiences with simulations, and the possibility of creating models of fundamental math/ science/technology processes. Like the best teachers, different forms of to-day's information technology can increase everybody's capacity to learn.

The question of the week might be this: "What is the role of media in our society?" A more intriguing and controversial question is the following: "How do you have a just society when genetics is so unjust?" The teacher has to make sure that everyone has an online study partner and that students know how to prepare a summary of their homework discussions.

Not many of us can easily juggle all of today's demands and integrate the results into the curriculum. But with time, practice, and a little in-service training, teachers less familiar with technology can easily become aware of the general issues and make the appropriate match between the problems they face and potential technological support needed.

Digital technology is transforming the social and educational environment before many of us have a chance to think carefully about what we hope to accomplish. Like everyone else, teachers are consumers of technology and they need to be able to judge critically the quality and usefulness of the electronic possibilities springing up around them.

Many people outside of school think that life today is moving too fast. They should try to imagine what it is like to be a teacher with new curriculum choices, political demands, standardized tests, and whiz-bang technologies swirling around them.

If you think the past is strange, try the future.

—Anonymous

Comprehending Video Messages

Parents, teachers, and other adults can significantly affect what information children gather from digital media. The skills learned from analyzing any visually intensive medium today will apply to more advanced multimedia platforms tomorrow. To become critical viewers who are literate about media messages, students should be able to do the following:

- Understand the grammar and syntax of television as expressed in different program forms
- Analyze the pervasive appeals of television advertising
- Compare similar presentations or those with similar purposes in different media
- Identify values in language, characterization, conflict resolution, and sound/visual images
- Identify elements in dramatic presentations associated with the concepts of plot, storyline, theme, characterizations, motivation, program formats, and production values
- Utilize strategies for the management of duration of viewing and program choices

Understanding media has to begin very early. Parents and teachers can engage in activities that affect children's interest in televised messages—and help them learn how to process video information. Good modeling behavior, explaining content, and showing how the program content relates to student interests are just a few examples of how adults can provide positive viewing motivation. Adults can also exhibit an informed response, point out misleading media messages, and take care not to build curiosity for undesirable programs (Zuckerberg, 2013a, 2013b).

The media habits of families play a large role in determining how children approach any medium. The length of time parents spend watching television, the kinds of programs viewed, and the reactions of parents and siblings toward programming messages all have a large influence on the child. If adults read and there are books, magazines, and newspapers around the house, children will pay more attention to print. Influencing what children may do online may be done with rules about what may or may not be watched, interactions with children during viewing, and the modeling of certain content choices.

It is increasingly clear that the education of children is a shared responsibility. Parents need connections with what is going on in the schools. But it is *teachers* who will be the ones called upon to make the educational connections entwining varieties of print and visual media with science, mathematics, or technology.

ACTIVITIES THAT CAN HELP STUDENTS MAKE
SENSE OF VISUAL MESSAGES

1. Help Students Critically View What They Watch

Decoding visual stimuli and learning from visual images require practice. Seeing an image does not automatically ensure learning from it. Students must be guided in decoding and looking critically at what they view. One technique is to have students "read" the image on various levels. Students identify individual elements and classify them into various categories, and then relate the whole to their own experiences, drawing inferences and creating new conceptualizations from what they have learned.

Encourage students to look at the plot and storyline. Identify the message of the program. What symbols (camera techniques, motion sequences, setting, lighting, etc.) does the program use to make its message? What does the director do to arouse audience emotion and participation in the story? What metaphors and symbols are used?

2. Compare Print and Video Messages

Have students follow a current event on the evening news and compare it to the same event written in a major newspaper. A question for discussion may be the following: How do the major newspapers influence what appears on a national network's news program? Encourage comparisons between both media. What are the strengths and weaknesses of each? What are the reasons behind the different presentations of a similar event?

3. Evaluate TV Viewing Habits

After compiling a list of their favorite TV programs, assign students to analyze the reasons for their popularity and examine the messages these programs send to their audience. Do the same for favorite books, magazines, newspapers, films, songs, and computer programs. Look for similarities and differences among different media forms.

4. Use Video for Instruction

Using digital tools, make three- to five-minute video segments to illustrate different points. This is often better than showing long videotapes or a film on a video cassette. For example, teachers can show a five-minute segment from a video cassette movie to illustrate how one scene uses foreshadowing or music to set up the next scene.

5. Analyze Advertising Messages

Advertisements provide a wealth of examples for illustrating media messages. Move students progressively from advertisements in print to television commercials, allowing them to locate features (such as packaging, color, and images) that influence consumers and often distort reality. Analyze and discuss commercials in children's TV programs: How many minutes of TV ads appear in an hour? How have toy manufacturers exploited the medium? What is the broadcasters' role? What should be done about it?

6. Create a Scrapbook of Media Clippings

Have students keep a scrapbook of newspaper and magazine clippings on television and its associates. Paraphrase text, draw a picture, or map out a personal interpretation of the articles. Share these with other students.

7. Create New Images from the Old

Have students take rather mundane photographs and multiply the image, or combine them with others, in a way that makes them interesting. Through the act of observing, it is possible to build a common body of experiences, humor, feeling, and originality. And through collaborative efforts, students can expand on ideas and make the group process come alive.

8. Use Debate for Critical Thought

Debating is a communications model that can serve as a lively facilitator for concept building. Taking a current and relevant topic and formally debating it can serve as an important speech/language extension. For example, the class can discuss how mass media can support political tyranny, public conformity, or the technological enslavement of society. The discussion can serve as a blend of social studies, science, and humanities studies. You can also build the process of writing or videotaping from the brainstorming to the final production stage.

9. Include Newspapers, Magazines, Literature, and Electronic Media (Like Brief Television News Clips) in Daily Class Activities

Use of the media and literature can enliven classroom discussion of current conflicts and dilemmas. Neither squeamish nor politically correct, these sources of information provide readers with something to think and talk about. And they can present the key conflicts and dilemmas of our time in a way that allows students to enter the discussion. These stimulating sources of information can help the teacher structure lessons that go beyond facts to stimulate reading, critical thinking, and thoughtful discussion. By not concealing adult disagreements, everyone can take responsibility for promoting understanding—engaging others in moral reflection and providing a coherence and focus that help turn controversies into advantageous educational experiences.

How to Choose Computer-based Activities

Most teachers subscribe to a number of professional journals, and just about every school staff room has dozens. The journals are simple enough to give to upper-grade students so that they can help with the selection. Many contain software reviews that can keep you up to date. Both paper and online educational technology magazines often publish an annotated list of what their critics take to be the best new programs of the year.

District supervisors of science and mathematics may have a list of what they think will work at your grade level. Of course, you can get your class directly involved in the software evaluation process. This helps your students reach the goal of understanding the educational purpose of the activity. We like to start our workshops by having teachers work in pairs to review a few good programs that most school districts actually have. As you and your students go about choosing programs for the classroom, the following checklist may prove useful:

1. Can the software or app be used easily by two students working together? (Graphic and spoken instructions help.)
2. What is the activity trying to teach, and how does it fit into the curriculum?
3. Do activities encourage students to experiment and think creatively about what they are doing?
4. Is it lively and interesting?

5. Does it allow students to collaborate, explore, and laugh?
6. Is the software technically sophisticated enough to build on multisensory ways of learning?
7. Is there any way to assess student performance?
8. What activities, materials, or manipulatives would extend the skills taught by this program?

The bottom line is this: *Do you and your students like it?* We suggest that teachers reserve their final judgment until they observe students in action. Do not expect perfection. But if it does not build on the unique capacities of the computer, then you may just have an expensive electronic workbook that will not be of much use to anybody.

With today's digital universe, there is every reason to expect science and math programs to be able to invite students to interact with creatures and phenomena from the biological and physical universe. Students can move from the past to the future and actively inquire about everything from experiments with dangerous substances to simulated interaction with long-dead scientists. Just do not leave out experiments with real chemicals and experiences with live human beings.

Good educational software often tracks individual progress over time and gives special attention to problem areas. Most of what you find online does not do that. Free Internet offerings have cut into the sale of educational software and diminished program quality. Another change is a tendency to move away from the computer platform and put educational programming on all kinds of gadgets.

As we venture out onto the electronic road ahead, we should remember the words of T. S. Eliot:

> Time present and time past are both perhaps contained in time future,
> And time future contained in time past.

NETWORKING TECHNOLOGIES

There are studies that point to some potential benefits when students and teachers use new computer-based technologies and information networks. For example:

- Computer-based simulations and laboratories can be downloaded and help support national standards (especially in subjects like science and math) by involving students in active- and inquiry-based learning.
- Networking technology, like the Internet, can help bring schools and homes closer together.
- Technology and telecommunications can help include students with a wide range of disabilities in regular classrooms.
- Distance learning, through networks like the Internet, can extend the learning community beyond the classroom walls.
- The Internet may help teachers continue to learn while also sharing problems/solutions with colleagues around the world. (Ohler, 2001)

Since the "Net" is rarely censored, it is important to supervise student work or use a program that blocks adult concerns. We suggest that teachers keep an eye on what students are doing and make sure that the classroom is offline when a substitute teacher is in.

Teachers may wish to communicate with peers, parents, and the larger world community. (However, we suggest not accepting instant messages from students and reserving your personal e-mail address for professional activities.)

In today's world, children grow up interacting with electronic media as much as they interact with print or people. They may be engaged. But does this mean that they are learning anything meaningful or that they are making good use of either educational *or* leisure time?

The Internet, like other electronic media, can distract students from direct interaction with peers—inhibiting important group, literacy, and physical exercise activities. The future may be bumpy, but it does not have to be gloomy. Good use of any learning tool depends on the strength and capacity of teachers. The best results occur when informed educators drive change rather than the technology itself.

Sailing through the crosscurrents of a technological age means harmonizing the present and the future, which means much more than reinventing the schools. It calls for attending to support mechanisms. Successfully sailing through the crosscurrents of our transitional age requires the development of habits of the heart and habits of the intellect. Thinking about the educational process has to precede thinking about the technology.

Possibilities for intelligent use of the computer-based technologies may be found in earlier media. For example, when television first gained a central place in the American consciousness, the sociologist Leo Bogart wrote that it was a "neutral instrument in human hands. It is and does what people want." The same thing might be said about today's multimedia and telecommunications technologies. The Internet and other computer-controlled educational tools may have great promise. But anyone who thinks that technological approaches will solve the problems of our schools is mistaken.

DIFFERENTIATION, TECHNOLOGY, AND INTERESTING GROUP WORK

For excellence, the presence of others is always required.

—Hannah Arendt

Differentiation, collaborative learning, and the Internet are natural partners. An example of a simple differentiated lesson for mixed-ability groups: Everyone reads or does the same science, math, or technology problem, activity, or section of text. Each student finds a partner and does some Internet research that he or she will bring back to the small group.

We sometimes have upper-grade students explore new media by going online to read reviews of related books. "Disruptive technology" is a good topic for student exploration. Disruptive technology, like improved search engines (Google), shakes things up by changing the way that students, adults, and businesses operate. Advertising and price comparisons change business practices. Information from the *outside* world is readily available for students. And individuals can download gene patterns to get information about the world *inside*.

Activities That Can Help Students Discover Technological Marvels

1. Explore the Magic of 3D Printers

One fascinating technological development is the availability of three-dimensional (3D) printers for creating objects. This is a research project that is guaranteed to blow the minds of your students away. Have student teams of three or four students research "3D printers."

Though not an entirely new concept since they have been used years back to make spare parts for cars and airplanes, 3D printers work by threading spools of plastic filament onto a heated nozzle that drops liquid plastic or any other material onto a surface layer by layer until the desired object is formed according to the design specification (O'Leary, 2013).

3D printers have been known to be able to make just about anything—from hard-to-find car parts for a 1966 Mustang to replacement parts for IKEA furniture products, to tiles for the Scrabble game, to adapters that will enable kids to connect their Duplo and Brio wooden train sets. A company called Crayon Creatures now has a product that will convert a child's drawing into a three-dimensional toy.

3D printers could be great to get students to design, invent, and prototype objects right in the classroom. Teachers from all over are excited by this possibility. In addition to engineers, many teachers have attended a recent 3D printing conference in New York, understandably expectant of great instructional possibilities. Justin Levinson, a New York technology consultant, aptly said, "It's not about printing. It's about how you start to look at the world. . . . You start to think, 'I can solve my own problems'" (O'Leary, 2013).

There are caveats attached to the availability of 3D printers—now fairly knowledgeable hobbyists can build guns using 3D printers. Think of what havoc this can bring to society.

Students who are interested in experimenting with 3D printers are best advised to find a hobbyist or a professional who can guide them in the process. Some libraries are even beginning to make 3D printers available, along with instructional help. These printers will not be hard to find—in the United States, Staples will be offering 3D printing services in their stores, and Amazon.com has started selling 3D printers and accessories. Then there are websites like Thingiverse that offers a repository of usable designs for such things as nuts and bolts, washers, a coat hook for the Volvo C30, a part for the Bugaboo stroller, and so forth.

You might want to lobby for the purchase of such a printer in your school. Two models recommended by *Make Magazine* as reliable and easy to use are the following: the Afinia H-Series ($1,599) or the Cube printer from 3-D Systems ($1,299) (O'Leary, 2013).

There are provocative issues around 3D printers. Ask student teams to think about the following issues—better yet, have them pose their own concerns:

- What do you think 3D printers will do to our manufacturing industries?
- What do you think 3D printers will do for consumers?

- Are there any disadvantages to having 3D printers available?
- Should the use of 3D printers be regulated by government?

2. *Looking Through Google Glass*

Another compelling team technology project would be to ask the students to research "Google Glass," which facilitates instant information exchange and sharing. David Pogue, the in-resident technology expert of the *New York Times*, considers this a true breakthrough product, even if it is only it in its pilot stage (Pogue, 2012).

A full-blown computer, Google Glass has been designed to be very light, wearable, and hands free, looking like a headband of a pair of glasses that hooks on your ears and lies along the eyebrow line. The screen is a small transparent block that sits above, to the right of the wearer's right eye. The design genius behind packing so much technology within a very small space is quite amazing. One can find the following items inside the right earpiece: memory, a processor, a camera, speaker and microphone, Bluetooth and Wi-Fi antennas, accelerometer, gyroscope, and a battery.

Google plans to add a cellular radio in a future version that will allow the user to get online instantly; right now, the device needs to tie in wirelessly with one's cellphone for online connectivity. What impressed Pogue the most is the fact that the small screen is completely invisible when one is preoccupied with some other task—talking, driving, or reading. But once the user focuses on this screen, the display is amazingly immersive, making one feel that he or she is gazing at a sizeable laptop screen.

The software that controls the device is activated by swiping the finger on the right earpiece in different directions, much like a touchpad. There is no keyboard or touchscreen. Different swiping directions guide the user through simple menus. Tapping is used to select the option you want. Speech recognition is also available for controlling the device. For example, if you say, "OK, Glass," the main menu will come up. You could issue verbal commands to take a picture or record a video: "OK, Glass, record a video." The device is still under development, and apps still need to be created for it.

Since the initial noncommercial version of the Google Glass is pricey at U.S.$1,500 and students may not be able to buy it, they can still get a sense of how it works by watching videos of pioneer end users on YouTube or some other Internet source. Have student teams discuss the following issues or generate their own questions:

- What are the major advantages of Google Glass for end users?
- What are the major disadvantages of Google Glass for end users?
- Will Google Glass encourage dangerous multitasking?
- Under what conditions should the use of Google Glass be encouraged?
- What are the implications of Google Glass on citizen privacy?
- Should the use of Google Glass be regulated by the government? What features of this device should be regulated and why?

3. How Far Should We Go with "Big Data" and "Data Mining"?

The other major technological development is that of "big data" and "data mining." Through the years, the cost of different forms of information technologies has declined, while its power and capabilities have increased. One of those capabilities is its ability to capture, store, process, and distribute data. Before we even used the phrase "big data," different kinds of organizations, whether private firms or public government agencies, used information technology for capturing and storing data they generated in order for them to do their work.

As the years progressed, the need and demand for storing more and more data just increased. As of today, there have been many other technologies, especially those enabled by the Internet, deployed in the marketplace that have contributed to an explosion on data—thus the term "big data." This phrase refers to the following sources of data, which are normally not associated with the regular operations of private businesses and government agencies: social networking data created by members of Facebook, MySpace, LinkedIn, Twitter, and so forth; data generated by sensors attached to houses, appliances, airplanes, cars, manufacturing equipment, and so forth; medical data generated by procedures like x-rays, special medical lab tests, and so forth; and the list goes on.

Collecting and storing data is meaningless if end users cannot make any sense out of it. Thus, we have "data mining," which refers to the use of analytical software employing both simple and complex statistical techniques in order to interpret the data, make useful predictions, and arrive at unexpected insights.

Most companies, for instance, use data mining on their customer-purchasing data in order to predict if their top customers will buy the latest car model now in the design stage. The U.S. government is using data mining, allegedly, for more "nefarious" purposes: "The NSA [National Security Agency] . . . keeps track of phone calls, monitors communications, and analyzes people's thoughts through data mining of Google searches and other online activity" (Bamford, 2013). The justification of the U.S. government for doing so is to protect its citizens from possible planned terrorist attacks.

Have student teams research data mining and what it means for consumers and citizens of a country. Think of issues relevant to data mining and have students reflect on dilemmas similar to those provoked by the following questions:

- Is the U.S. government justified in monitoring citizen's phone calls and Internet activities in order to gather data that could be useful for protecting against terrorist attacks?
- What are beneficial uses of data mining for society?
- What are harmful uses of data mining for society?

After discussions in small collaborative groups, projects or work assignments can be brought back to the whole class, and each group can share its findings. Sometimes group members may want to put their findings online or post their book reviews at Amazon.com. Wikipedia has open editing, so students can put some things there. This online encyclopedia is very timely, but the accuracy is mixed. So we tell students that it is a good starting point, but that it should not be their only source.

As a close associate of problem solving, math and collaborative inquiry in science technology–based instruction is dramatically changing how students and teachers go about doing their work. New technologies give teachers powerful tools for offering a customized curriculum in a social context. The digital *Thinking Readers*, for example, are full-text computerized books that provide built-in supports that include individualized learning and reciprocal (student-to-student) teaching. We like using "know/want to know/learned" (KWL) charts with them. These charts have three columns labeled *know*, *want to know*, and *learned*. Just before reading, two students work together to put down what they know about a subject. In the second column, they write what they want to know. After they explored a math- or science-related passage, they write what they learned in the third column. This builds on prior knowledge and teamwork. It also brings a focus to the work. To communicate the work to everybody, we sometimes have student partnerships put their work on large pieces of paper so that they can be taped up, explained, and seen by everybody in a whole-class discussion.

When it comes to engaging all students using digital technology, it is important to provide multiple options—like practicing skills, accessing information, and working with peers to engage with math and science materials. It is also important to go well beyond lectures and printed materials because they can fail to reach some students—especially underachieving students.

Collaborative groups are another way to help less motivated students by encouraging them to take on different roles, share resources, and help themselves and others learn. Although technology has something to offer, it takes a commitment to critical thinking, social interaction, and at least some hard work to learn math and science.

When students are actively engaged with ideas and other students, the natural power of teamwork accommodates more types of learning than the old chalk-and-teacher-talk model. It has always been true that when interesting questions are raised in learning groups, those involved tend to lead each other forward. Struggling students may need to take conscious steps to activate prior knowledge. This can be done as a small group reviews what has been covered out loud and on paper.

Collaborative learning is effective because the framework of the strategy is good for all students. The research also suggests that somewhat collaborative learning groups result in more cross-cultural friendships and have some positive effect on intergroup relations (NSTA et al., 2013). With an increasingly diverse student talent pool, learning to advance through the intersection of different points of view is more important than ever.

While aiming high, teachers have to be realistic about what children and young adults can achieve. A major goal at every level involves generating more enthusiasm for mathematical problem solving and scientific (collaborative) inquiry. To help *all* students, teachers need to focus on the concept(s) that they want to teach. The next step is figuring out how different kinds of learners are going to show an understanding of the concepts covered.

When it comes to active small-group learning, it takes the right mix of students, because one child with a serious emotional problem can undo a group—or even the whole class. In general, mixed-ability groups work well.

The social integration of disinterested students with those who are doing well with math and science gives many of them their best chance to flourish. But remember, it is just as bad to say that Jane is bored as to say that Johnny cannot do math or science. So teachers must provide extra enrichment for their high-achieving students so that they stay challenged and their parents stay cooperative.

Language makes us human
Math, science, and technology make us powerful
And being in community with others can make us free.

—Dennis Adams

Technological Possibilities That Include All Students

Besides altering how we learn, play, live, and work, technology has become a powerful tool for doing mathematics and science. It can help puncture some of the colorful balloons of pseudoscience and mathematical nonsense. But if our faith in technology simply becomes a powerful ideology, we miss the point. It can be magical, but it is not the main purpose in life or a silver bullet for educational improvement.

Technology is an important thing, but not the only thing. If computer-based learning is to be healthy, then we have to ask some challenging questions about it. A little skepticism will improve the product. Experienced teachers know that educational shortcuts from filmstrips to videotapes have promised a lot and delivered little or nothing. Digital technology promises more. But to paraphrase Jane Austen, *when unquestioned vanity goes to work on a weak mind, it produces every kind of mischief.*

Applications derived from math and science help drive technology and technology returns the favor. Technology expands as mathematics and science call for more sophisticated instrumentation and techniques to study phenomena that are unobservable by other means due to danger, quantity, speed, size, or distance. As technology provides tools for investigations of the natural world, it expands mathematical and scientific knowledge beyond preset boundaries.

Doing a good job in today's classroom environment requires teachers who can help students from diverse backgrounds gain the competencies needed for identifying, analyzing, and solving mathematical, scientific, and technological problems. Fully understanding the art and science of teaching means knowing how to generate good questions and recognizing when to move in the direction of student interest.

With the explosion of high-tech possibilities, it is important to remember that curriculum connections to the world of numbers and nature must be filtered through the mind of the teacher.

Teachers need to convey some excitement about expanding subject matter. To get their students more engaged with math and science, it takes all the technological help that they can get. It helps if you soften subject matter boundaries and engage underachieving students in a study of the physical and biological universe.

Like the fields of mathematics and science, technological and social progress is usually incremental. Of course, there are times when things flip overnight. But spectacular new approaches and theories are relatively rare events and will continue to be so. Regardless of whether change is fast or slow, an understanding of and ability to use technological tools are necessary to live, learn, and work in an increasingly complex and technological world.

With just about any subject, it is best if educators go beyond one-shot assignments and weave technological possibilities into the fabric of the class-room. Along the way, teachers can use the full range of available technology to enhance their productivity and improve their professional practice.

Scripts and specific instructional models cannot replace teacher creativity, spontaneity, and practicality. A little rule bending goes well with high-quality teaching. When seasoned professionals are supported and well prepared, they can walk in the world with such confidence and enthusiasm that they do not have to fear the unsettling effects of change.

SUMMARY, CONCLUSION, AND LOOKING AHEAD

Changes in the academic competition and the world economy keep raising the bar for what our students have to achieve. Staying at the same level of educational achievement, or getting just a little better, just is not good enough. Yes, we do have some great schools that meet the most stringent international standards, but there are not enough of them.

Even before children enter school, their level of readiness depends upon the language used by parents and caretakers. For example, the number of words spoken by more educated parents vastly exceeds the number spoken by less educated parents (Rosenberg, 2013). So unless there is some pre-school intervention, the end result is having some children already way behind before they even start school.

The new guidelines in math, science, and technology suggest that our schools must be better at improving the performance of students who struggle with these subjects. A major goal is making sure that all students become more intelligent consumers of math and science. This means learning critical thinking skills and becoming more engaged with these subjects.

Up-to-date practice includes connecting content standards to practice in a way that cuts across grade levels to build on prior learning, teamwork, and promoting real-world applications (Evenson et al., 2013). In the hands of competent teachers, technology is a powerful lever for adding power to instruction. It can amplify learning and motivate both high-achieving and underachieving students.

Computers and the Internet give us access to more people, more information, and more practical knowledge. At the moment a combination of online lessons and hybrid (in-class) assignments have value. But face-to-face human communication is essential for developing critical thinking, teamwork skills, and the motivation for advancing the well-being of individuals and the community.

With or without technology, the desired outcomes of education still have a lot to do with going beyond technical and practical applications to develop the whole person. This includes the cultivation of the imagination, cultural sensitivities, and intellectual curiosity. In our collective future, developing the ability to learn new things, innovate, and engage civically trumps utilitarian (job skills) training any day.

Educators are finding themselves focusing more than ever on how they can enhance learning for students who come from a variety of family backgrounds, economic situations, and linguistic environments. In the United States, for example, poor students are doing worse than they did thirty years ago, middle-class students are doing about the same, and students from wealthy families are doing better than ever (Noah, 2013).

The reasons for educational inequality have a lot to do with increasing income inequality, tax structure, government policy, and the erosion of funding for education. Other non-school factors include the following: the community environment, the rising costs of health care, and the lack of a serious industrial policy regarding the effects of automation.

In tomorrow's schools, learners will be even more economically, socially, culturally, and educationally diverse than they are today. A key motivator is bound to be using a variety of instructional models that draw upon technology, group collaboration, and the learning dispositions of students.

The faster ultramodern technology and its online associates become, the more classical attributes matter. Good judgment, critical thinking, intellectual curiosity, and the basic values of right and wrong cannot be downloaded. Positive values must be uploaded by parents, teachers, and the students themselves.

Subject matter knowledge is one thing, but teachers also have to design, motivate, and adjust learning. Using the best practices fluently and flexibly is part of the job description. The same can be said for knowing the characteristics of effective instruction.

There is little question that in the hands of the thoughtful and well informed, technological tools can be powerful levers. Both low- and high-tech applications can enhance lessons. The key is making the connections among content, technology, and what is actually happening in the classroom.

For teachers to lead students into a future that is useful, all the available tools must be used to orchestrate learning conditions in a way that brings out the best in everybody. It is educators, after all, who must make appropriate choices about technology systems, subject matter, resources, and services. And it is teachers who must implement a variety of instructional and grouping strategies in a way that meets the needs of all learners.

The future is always more peculiarly strange than any of our tidy imaginings.
—Gregory Rawlings

QUESTIONS FOR TEACHERS AND PROSPECTIVE TEACHERS

1. What are the possibilities and pitfalls associated with a society that is often overwhelmed by technology? Give some good and bad possibilities for a technology-driven future.
2. What is the most useful and unique thing you have heard about technology recently? Name some myths and some magic.
3. What roles do play, passion, and purpose have in relation to learning about math, science, and technology?
4. How does technology erode the edges of personal privacy?
5. How might technology empower and inform your students?
6. Could you explain two successes, one failure, and a funny result that you have had with helping students understand the implications of digital technology?

REFERENCES AND RESOURCES

Bamford, J. (2013). "They Know Much More Than You Think." *New York Times*, *The New York Review of Books*, August 15.

Benjamin, A. (2005). *Differentiated Instruction Using Technology: A Guide for Middle and High School Teachers*. Larchmont, NY: Eye On Education, Inc.

Bers, M. (2007). *Blocks to Robots: Learning with Technology in Early Childhood Classrooms*. New York, NY: Teachers College Press.

Cathcart, G. S., Pothier, Y. M., Vance, J. H., & Bezuk, N. S. (2010). *Learning Mathematics in Elementary and Middle Schools: A Learner-Centered Approach.* 5th ed. Boston, MA: Pearson Education.

Evenson, A., McIver, M., Schwols, A., & Kendall, J., eds. (2013). *Common Core Standards for Elementary Grades 3–5 Math & English Language Arts Learners: A Quick-Start Guide.* Alexandra, VA: Association for Supervision and Curriculum Development.

International Educational Technology Association. (2000). *Standards for Technological Literacy: Content for the Study of Technology.* Reston, VA: International Educational Technology Association.

Lanier, J. (2013). *Who Owns the Future.* New York, NY: Penguin.

McTighe, J., & Wiggens, G. (2013). *Essential Questions: Opening Doors to Student Understanding.* Alexandria, VA: Association for Supervision and Curriculum Development.

Morozov, E. (2012). *To Save Everything Click Here: The Folly of Technological Solutionism.* New York, NY: Public Affairs Books.

National Research Council. (2000). *National Science Education Standards.* Washington, DC: National Academy Press.

Noah, T. (2013). *The Great Divergence: America's Growing Inequality Crisis and What We Can Do About It.* New York, NY: Bloomsbury.

NSTA. (2013). *Next Generation Science Standards.* Washington, DC: National Science Teachers Association, American Association for the Advancement of Science, National Research Council, and Achieve.

Ohler, J. (2001). *Future Courses: A Compendium of Thought About Education, Technology, and the Future.* Bloomington, IN: TECHNOS Press of the Agency for Instructional Technology.

O'Leary, A. (2013). "3-D Printers to Make Things You Need or Like." *New York Times*, June 19.

Pogue, D. (2012). "Google Glass and the Future of Technology." *New York Times*, September 13.

Rawlings, G. (1996). *Moths to the Flame.* Cambridge, MA: MIT Press.

Rosenburg, T. (2013). *Join the Club: How Peer Pressure Can Transform the World.* New York, NY: W. W. Norton.

Schiller, F. (1954). *Aesthetic Education.* New Haven, CT: Yale University Press.

Thompson, C. (2013). *Smarter than You Think: How Technology Is Changing Our Minds for the Better.* New York, NY: HarperCollins.

Wenglinsky, H. (2005). *Using Technology Wisely: The Keys to Success in Schools.* New York, NY: Teachers College Press.

Zuckerberg, R. (2013a). *Dot Complicated.* New York, NY: HarperOne/HarperCollins.

Zuckerberg, R. (2013b). *DOT.* New York, NY: HarperOne/HarperCollins. (Picture book: ages 4 to 8)